CONTENTS

C000291949

1   The Silbury enigma.

2   The history.   8

    1968. Atkinson and the BBC.   15

    May 2000. The inevitable calamity.   22

3   The theories.   25

4   The landscape shapes an idea.   35

5   In the field.   40

    The view from Silbury Hill.   40

    Intervisibility of monuments.   42

    Territorial boundaries.   45

    The astronomy.   56

    Silbury Hill and Marlborough Mount.   57

6   The final intervention.   62

7   Revelation.   69

8   Some pre-Silbury Silburys.   85

9   Conclusion.   124

    Appendix.   129

    Bibliography.   132

    Index.   136

He's a hawthorn, a raven, a scarecrow, a haven
For moon blessed thought and opinion
He will laugh like the fountains, the bones of the mountains
Lie deep in his forest religion.

AL STEWART – *Zero she flies*

THE SILBURY REVELATION

Part 1. The Silbury enigma.

Picture 1. Silbury Hill.

The poignant remains of our prehistoric heritage are testament to the dawning of British civilisation over three and a half millennia before the Roman invasion and the Christian era. Consider that around 1,500 years from now in the year 3500 AD, the Roman occupation of Britain will be as far back in time as the origins of our megalithic culture were to the Romans.

That thought usually puts things into perspective for me, and increases my wonder at the achievements of the ancient Britons. In a time before the wheel, they could transport and then erect stones up to 100 tonnes in weight, and quarry colossal amounts of material as hard as rock with nothing more than deer antlers. Even more impressively, somehow, they were motivated to do so throughout these islands.

Unfortunately for generations of schoolchildren including myself, as Alistair Moffat wrote in his wonderfully informative and insightful *Before Scotland* (Thames and Hudson 2005), "Until very recently our curricula (an apposite Latin borrowing) and examination systems were devised by people whose education had been based on Roman and Greek principles." The result was that even the acknowledgement, let alone the study of our ancient monuments, was simply too inconvenient for an educational system and a society that fostered the patently absurd notion that British civilisation commenced with the relatively recent and totalitarian regime of the Romans.

Something that possibly could be said to have begun with them, and that increased in fervour as Christianity took a stranglehold during the medieval period, was the dismantling, demonising and usurping of our ancient sites. Some had disparaging place names attached to them such as 'Devil's Den' or 'Devil's Quoits', and many more were either systematically destroyed or pillaged for building materials. At some of the old meeting places such as stone circles, churches were built to encourage continuity of attendance under new mentorship. We will never know how many of the pagan sites have gone without trace, but the ancient British culture was as old and enduring as its revered hills, and it could not be suppressed forever.

More liberal attitudes began to form in the 1960s, and since then, interest in 'prehistory', its monuments and alternative ideologies relating to them has mushroomed. Now, the monuments exert a powerful hold on our imaginations. Of course, it is the air of mystery of many of these sites that we find so captivating, as little is known about their true meaning or purpose.

Archaeology has provided basic facts from which the sites can be assessed in terms of dating and sometimes even of usage. At some sites those facts are unambiguous, creating boundaries within which there is little scope for misinterpretation. At others, the parameters are far wider. For many among us this presents opportunities to escape from the mundane realities of life, and the ancient sites are proclaimed to be proof of long-lost super-civilisations or even alien visitation. More realistically, for most observers it is the sheer time and effort that was so clearly invested in the great megalithic and earthwork constructions of the Late Stone Age that is so beguiling. That is particularly true of the awe-inspiring monuments constructed during the Late Neolithic period up to the transition with the Copper or Bronze Age, such as Avebury henge and Stonehenge. In the hypnotic presence of these mighty stones, banks and ditches, we can be led to believe that the motivation, collective will and cooperation necessary to achieve such feats is evidence of a former egalitarian society that calls to us through the ages and tugs at our heartstrings. Is that simply because we wish it so, or is there some truth in a Neolithic 'golden age' when people were attuned to the energies of land and sky; living in harmony with nature not only by necessity, but also through understanding and religious conviction?

Most archaeologists and prehistorians would answer that question with a resounding "NO", barely disguising their frustration with meddling romantics. "Sheer speculation and wishful thinking" they would say, and quite rightly so; they are scientists, and as such they must be custodians of the facts. I fully appreciate their contempt for many alternative theories that are based largely on misinformation, and often in blatant contradiction of clear evidence. Nevertheless, there are times when archaeologists' interpretations of the facts can be equally frustrating.

Even the most conservative of them accept that many Neolithic monuments served some astronomical/calendrical purpose, and that the sites were essentially ritualistic. The general assumption is that Neolithic 'science' was interwoven with religion. For example, it is universally held that Stonehenge (a cremation cemetery) was deliberately aligned on the Summer Solstice sunrise/Winter Solstice sunset axis, or if you prefer, the longest day and the longest night. There also appear to be lunar orientations within some of its stone settings and in very early postholes in its north-eastern sector. A very strong case can be made that the famous Heelstone is actually aligned to a lunar event, and definitely not the summer sunrise as is popularly believed.

Recent publications have ably demonstrated that at Stonehenge there appears to have been a distinction between east as the domain of 'day and the living', and west as the domain of 'night and the ancestors'. Many other circles, particularly in Scotland, are accepted to have lunar orientations. I believe lunar orientation to be true of *all* stone circles – but that's another story. Certain long barrows and other 'tombs' (they are clearly much more than merely tombs) also appear to be astronomically aligned.

For the Neolithic population, life, death and the cosmos appear to have been interrelated. So, we do at least have some clues to the meanings and usages of their sites, although there is one particular Neolithic monument that until now has defied all attempts at understanding. It is the mother of all ancient British mysteries and an integral part of the wonderful Avebury/Stonehenge World Heritage Site. I refer of course to Silbury Hill; the largest prehistoric man-made mound in Europe.

Today, the mound looms high above the busy A4 road from London to the West Country in the heart of the North Wiltshire Downs. The mound and its close neighbour Avebury henge belong to one of the most intricate Neolithic complexes in Europe, clustered around the upper reaches of the River Kennet and its Winterbourne tributaries. The partially re-erected henge contains remnants of the largest stone circle in the world, and the world's largest hilltop causewayed enclosure is found in the same valley (or perhaps more accurately 'hollowed plateau') on Windmill Hill. At least two stone avenues, each over a mile in length, ran from the henge to other monuments. The largest and most numerous long barrows in Britain are in this locality, along with earthworks, the former sites of huge timber constructions known as palisaded enclosures and an inestimable number of lost standing stones.

Whatever the intentions of the builders, as centuries passed, the meaning of the complex as a whole and the mound in particular were lost. Archaeological attempts to restore our understanding of the mound began in 1776 with the latest ending in 2008. From the results of the investigations, we can say that approximately 4,500 years before modern-day Britons erected the ill-conceived Millennium Dome, the ancient Britons built a dome that was designed to stand for millennia.

We do not know how long the construction work took, but when the builders stood back to admire their handiwork, they would have seen something similar to how we see it today. That is, a conical mound 37 metres in height, around 28m wide at its flat top and approximately 167m in diameter at the base. That represents a construction of 239,000 cubic metres of material, the bulk of which is chalk that came from the surrounding quarry/ditch and the adjoining hillside at the mound's southern quarter. The hillside was steeply sculpted or 'scarped' to leave only two narrow causeways, presumably for access to the mound. The whole monument is estimated to have required three million man-hours to complete.

What the modern eye cannot see, but which obviously were known to the builders, are the astonishing interior design and methods of construction that made Silbury so enduring. Excavations carried out in the 1960s and the 2000s (all investigations described in Part 2) found that beneath its thin outer layer of crushed chalk and vegetation, the mound appears to be stabilised by a stepped series of radial and concentric chalk walls that would have rendered its frame similar in appearance to the stepped pyramids of ancient Egypt. It is also possible the 'steps' were in fact spirally constructed. Over the millennia since its construction some slippage of surface material has occurred, and now the mound is a little wider at the base where it joins the silted-up ditch.

At some time prior to the 17th century, a folk legend arose that a King Sil (or Zel) was buried on horseback somewhere within Silbury. Because of the legend and the fact that later Bronze Age round barrows are known to contain burials, until quite recently it had been reasonable to attribute a sepulchral purpose to the mound. Despite Silbury's unprecedented size and its unique location in a valley basin, it had been perceived as the mother of all round barrows. That idea remained in vogue until 1968 when Silbury's third major archaeological intervention failed to find any evidence at all of chambers or deliberately constructed hollows within its solidly built body. Within the last ten years, investigations utilising the most modern seismic survey equipment have confirmed that the only hollows in Silbury were caused by the interventions of archaeologists and the subsequent collapse of their tunnels, with the voids migrating upwards through the mound. Consequently, we have all been left completely in the dark as to why the great mound was ever built, and with only one exception, why it is so unlike any other Neolithic monument. Intriguingly, that sole exception stands just five miles from Silbury in the same river valley.

What could have motivated the people to construct such an enormous monument as Silbury Hill for no apparent reason? Clearly, it must have been something at the very core of their belief systems, and yet that belief does not appear to be manifest anywhere in Britain apart from the Avebury region: very strange.

Archaeologists have done their best to provide answers to the Silbury enigma, particularly in the last decade when they have done sterling work to repair damage to the mound caused by their predecessors. However, they can only report what they find, and those findings have served only to deepen the mystery. That has opened the floodgates to a plethora of alternative theories, largely inspired since the 1970s by the author Michael Dames who perceives Silbury as an Earth Goddess figure and harvest hill. Many writers, including Dames and perhaps most famously the archaeologist Marija Gimbutas, have presented persuasive arguments for a pan-European Neolithic Earth Goddess cult. More recently, that ideology has been supported by the inspirational work of the multi-talented Julian Cope (whose interest in megalithic culture lends an entirely new meaning to 'rock star'), with the result that many now perceive Silbury as the 'omphalos'; the navel or centre of the spiritual world. It is certainly a focal point for alternative beliefs. Understandably, archaeologists who care about their careers are reluctant to endorse such opinions.

At the time of writing, it is fully fourteen years since I moved to Swindon in order to indulge my fascination with the Avebury/Stonehenge complex and with Silbury Hill in particular. I was motivated to do so after observing the Neolithic monuments of Cumbria in their stunning landscapes whilst researching my hiking guidebooks. In those fourteen years, I have encountered and been assisted by many dedicated and knowledgeable people from both the scientific and alternative camps, and met others whose opinions were somewhat less helpful.

Anyone who has experienced the multi-ideological maelstrom of Avebury will know what I mean. Some archaeologists here are extremely conservative, while others are much more open-minded. There are amateur archaeological/historical research groups and individuals who share a great passion for the area's antiquities, and whose knowledge of them is positively encyclopaedic. That is in stark contrast to some of their fellow locals who would prefer that the monuments had never existed. The numerous crop-circle enthusiasts and ufologists are blissfully unaware of the terrestrial circle-makers all around them, while the earth energy dowsers and ley line hunters never seem to agree with each other. Not forgetting, of course, the various druid orders, from which two very colourful characters have proclaimed themselves 'Keeper of the Stones' and 'King Arthur'. Avebury can be exasperating, but never dull.

I did not expect that my project would take so long, but it is very difficult to maintain a disciplined approach and concentrate on any one particular aspect of the Avebury/Stonehenge World Heritage Site where there is so much to see and investigate. My endless diversions conspired to make the years slip by almost imperceptibly, and archaeological reports that seemed to take forever to be published were another drawback. Finally, after all the research and field work, it was sheer good fortune that showed me Silbury Hill in its true light. It should have been obvious from the very outset for someone with a background in observing landscapes, yet sometimes it is true that one cannot see the wood for the trees. The visionary Michael Dames was right to assert that Silbury should be considered a religious icon representing the Earth Mother, although he quite literally failed to see the wider picture, and when Julian Cope wrote of natural hill altars and sacred mother hills he came close, so very close to the ultimate answer.

Bear with me now through this brief account of Silbury's chequered history and the research it has inspired. I hope to demonstrate that all the archaeological intrusions the great mound has suffered have been unnecessary, for the answer to the Silbury enigma has always been hidden in plain sight.

Part 2. The history.

We owe a great debt to two antiquarians of the 17th and 18th centuries who rediscovered the practically forgotten Avebury prehistoric complex. Without John Aubrey and William Stukeley, it is conceivable the entire wonder would have been lost (Stukeley actually witnessed its destruction taking place). While it is true that Silbury and other Wiltshire hills were still celebrated locally as the venues for seasonal fairs and gatherings, it was because of Aubrey and Stukeley that the great mound gradually re-entered the national consciousness.

By 1663, John Aubrey was a Fellow of the Royal Society of London for the Improvement of Natural Knowledge, and as a Wiltshire man he had achieved a great familiarity with the antiquities of the region. The fact that he only discovered the Avebury complex by accident when out riding indicates just what a sorry state the monuments must have been in at that time. Many were obscured by buildings, and others had suffered centuries of neglect, overgrowth and deliberate destruction. Aubrey had informed the Royal Society that Avebury "did as much excel Stonehenge, as a cathedral does a parish church", and the Society conveyed his view to King Charles II. Subsequently, the king requested a guided tour of the area with Aubrey, who included a walk up Silbury in the itinerary. The king was so impressed that he instructed Aubrey to survey the entire complex, and Aubrey's plan of the Avebury monuments is still considered a masterpiece even though basic measurements of Silbury are missing. The reason is that Aubrey had been promised accurate measurements and volumes already taken by Sir Jonas Moore, Surveyor of the Ordnance. Unfortunately, upon Moore's death the papers were lost.

Aubrey included Silbury in his general plan of Avebury, depicting the mound's relationship with the henge, the avenues and other monuments. His plan is believed to contain the very first illustration of Silbury. Aubrey also was the first to write about the folk traditions of the mound, referring to the horseback burial of King Sil and to a curious belief that the hill was raised "whilst a posnet of milk was seething". A posnet is a cooking pot, so perhaps the folklore is suggesting that the mound was raised very quickly, literally in the time it takes to boil a pot of milk. Aubrey featured his work on Silbury in the enormously successful publication *Camden's Britannia*, and the mound's popularity and status were on the rise.

Then along came one William Stukeley, arguably England's greatest ever antiquarian. He spent long periods of time in and around Avebury, particularly in the summers of 1723 and 1724. A Lincolnshire doctor and clergyman, Stukeley was a genius in combining artistic skill with the precision of a surveyor. His drawings of the Avebury monuments placed them accurately within their landscape settings, with particular attention given to perspective of the monuments and the land from a host of vantage points. That is an extremely difficult skill to master, and although not infallible, Stukeley was certainly a master. He left a record of both Avebury and other prehistoric landscapes that are still published regularly, the importance of which will become evident later in these pages.

Stukeley's illustrations include a number that depict Silbury either as the principal subject or within the view from other monuments. Four of his drawings show the mound as a truncated cone, sometimes with indications of the still visible 'terrace' slightly below the summit. He noted that the mound was made of chalk, and that its material had probably been quarried from the surrounding ditch. Also, he described the two causeways that connect the mound to the scarped hillside at the southern quarter of the monument, and surmised that their purpose was to allow access for a large workforce. He was the first to propose there may be some significance to Silbury's very close proximity to the source of the River Kennet at Swallowhead Springs.

In 1723, the lord of Avebury Manor ordered the planting of trees on Silbury's flat summit, evidently as part of a designed landscape. Stukeley recorded that the workmen had dug up the body of *the great king* in a very shallow grave at the top (italics mine, presumably Stukeley was referring to the King Sil legend). The bones were rotten, crumbling in the workmen's fingers. John Fowler, one of the workmen, claimed to have recovered an extremely rusty iron chain from the digging, which he sold to Stukeley. It was this artefact more than anything else that moulded Stukeley's conviction the mound was prehistoric, as he believed the chain to be part of the bridle or harness of an Iron Age British king's chariot. In fact, the only illustration of the chain indicates it is from a horse-bit similar to those in use around the 11th century AD. Also, in his excitement, it seems that Stukeley had overlooked the improbability of a monarch being interred in an easily accessible location near the surface of such an imposing edifice. It wasn't long before Stukeley's claim to have identified the original burial was dismissed, although his conviction of a prehistoric date for the mound certainly stood the test of time. Stukeley's *Abury* was published in 1743, ensuring the enduring fame of Silbury Hill and the Avebury complex.

Stukeley certainly was not alone at the time in his belief that prehistoric Britain was led by druids; evidently, that was the prevailing opinion of his contemporaries. It appears that he got a little carried away by his enthusiasm for druidism, and took the druidic name 'Chynondax'. After that, his disciplined approach and attention to detail waned, with the result that his later drawings of the Avebury prehistoric complex took on druidic iconography that wasn't really there; infamously depicting the avenues, henge and Sanctuary circle as the tail, body and head of a druidic serpent. That did his reputation no good at all, particularly among modern archaeologists. It was not until 2003 that his reputation was restored when excavations discovered the long-lost Beckhampton Avenue of standing stones exactly where Stukeley said it would be (leading to the extant stones known locally as 'Adam and Eve'). Conventional opinion now is that Stukeley was indeed a genius who perhaps loved antiquity a little too much.

Edward Drax, a colonel in the Dorset militia, became the first person to instigate what could very loosely be described as an archaeological investigation into Silbury in 1776. He proposed to dig a vertical shaft through the centre of the mound to the old ground surface, almost certainly inspired to do so after reading of similar mounds on the Russian steppes that had produced quite fabulous grave goods. Drax first sought permission from the landowner Arthur Jones, and then set about securing the financial investment he needed. This was not immediately forthcoming from either the Royal Society or the Society of Antiquaries, so Drax approached the Duke of Northumberland, Sir Hugh Smithson Percy. The duke was well known for his interest in science and antiquities, and as a coalmine owner would have been well versed in mining methods.

Employing miners who probably came from the Kingswood Colliery near Bristol, Drax commenced to dig a shaft measuring 8 feet square at the centre of the summit. The first 6 feet of the excavation were found to be disturbed ground, probably the result of the Lord of the Manor's tree-planting 53 years earlier. Next, the original deposits were encountered, consisting of chalk blocks "the size of a man's head". On approaching the old ground surface, the miners discovered a perpendicular cavity approximately 15 centimetres in diameter. Initially, Drax concluded it was the hole left by a timber post that had rotted away. That is most likely the true explanation, for it is entirely conceivable the earliest deposits of the mound would have been piled up around a central post. Later, Drax became dissatisfied with such a prosaic explanation, and went on to suggest the mound may have been constructed over a sacred druid oak. That seems to have been a fanciful notion, as only a very young and unremarkable oak tree would have a trunk measuring 15 centimetres in diameter. A fragment of wood was discovered near the bottom of the shaft, which was probably a shard of the miners' own shoring planks. The miners also discovered pieces of deer antlers at regular intervals, but unfortunately for the colonel and the duke, that was the full extent of any buried treasure.

It is unclear whether any attempt was made to backfill the excavation. Miners at the time did not usually do so, and there are accounts of great mounds of spoil left around the monument. An illustration drawn in 1849 shows a very deep slump in the centre of Silbury, although a report by the amateur archaeologist Alfred Pass almost 40 years later stated that all the material appeared to have been refilled by Drax. 21st century events proved that Drax had not done so, and that his excavation was the first in a series of interventions that would ultimately prove almost disastrous.

For 73 years after the Drax investigation, Silbury Hill was left in peace. That ended in 1849 when the Royal Archaeological Institute hired the banker Richard Falkner and civil engineer Henry Blandford to investigate the mound and to drive a tunnel to its centre. They decided the best place to begin the excavation was from the western causeway in the southern quarter of the mound.

It is a common misconception that Silbury is entirely man-made owing to its smooth, conical appearance. In fact, it stands on a natural promontory that extends into low grassland in the deepest part of the upper valley. Although practically every archaeologist believes the promontory was sculpted to conform to the mound's conical shape after the mound was completed, there is actually no evidence for that, and it is not necessarily the case. What we can be sure of, is that in the mound's southern quarter, the original ground surface of the promontory is around 9 metres above the current base of the mound, and that the base conforms closely to the original level of the grassland surrounding the promontory. At the centre of the mound, the old ground level is around 7.5m above the base. If that gradient continues, the old ground level in the northern quarter would be 5 or 6m above the base, although a distinct change in the angle of slope on the northern side indicates that it may be a little higher.

It was below the original ground level near the western causeway that Blandford began to dig a tunnel approximately 2m tall and 1m wide. The tunnel inclined upwards and broke through the old ground surface after a distance of around 30m, to find the mound at that point was composed of brown earth and chalk rubble. Tunnelling continued to the mound's centre at an estimated distance of 49m from the entrance, and then continued a little further. At the very centre, the excavators found layers of undecayed turf, grass and moss lying one over the other, amongst which were freshwater shells.

At that point in time, the investigation was taken over by the Very Reverend John Merewether, Dean of Hereford Cathedral, and lateral excavations were made to both east and west of the centre. In one of the eastern excavations, sarsen stones were found "placed with their concave surface downwards, favouring the line of the heap" (the central stack of turves and mosses). On top of some of the stones, fragments of bone and the tine of a stag's antler had been placed. Merewether also observed "great quantities of moss still in a state of comparative freshness", and a dense black layer of organic material containing fragments of small branches that sealed the turf stack and emitted a peculiar smell. The smell is now believed to have been fungal contamination caused by the 1776 shaft.

One month into the dig both Falkner and Blandford threw in the trowel, leaving Merewether in charge. Two more tunnels were made, one of which came across the base of the 1776 shaft, and the other curved northwards following the line of the central stack of organic material. When Merewether left, work continued under the direction of the Reverend John Bathurst Deane. Finally, with the excavated chalk left lying in the ditch outside the entrance and no backfilling at all carried out, the tunnel was sealed by a brick wall. As a result, after two major and extremely damaging investigations, no treasure had been found, no tomb or chamber had been discovered, and most importantly, archaeology had no answers to the Silbury mystery. However, with the sepulchral theory of Silbury obviously discredited, the Royal Archaeological Institute submitted that Silbury "had some connection with the great temple of Avebury, either for the assembly of the people, or for religious purposes."

The next investigation took place in 1867, and can only be described as farcical. Over 140 years earlier, William Stukeley had pinpointed the course of a Roman road running to the south of Silbury. Despite that, and regardless of local archaeologists who could locate the road as an earthwork, one James Fergusson and the newly founded Wiltshire Archaeological and Natural History Society decided they were going to prove that Silbury was constructed over the Roman road. Fergusson believed that Avebury's monuments had been constructed to celebrate King Arthur's victory over the Saxons at the battle of Mount Badon, thus miscalculating the mound's true provenance by at least three millennia. His happy band dug trenches on the eastern side of the mound, where of course they found nothing of significance. Only then did they investigate the field to the south, where they found that the Roman road headed towards the mound and then curved away to avoid the southern ditch. Clearly, the Roman engineers had used Silbury in their sightlines, driving their road deep into the heart of one of pagan Britain's most revered monumental landscapes. As a political and military statement it could not have been more explicit, and it was something they repeated throughout the land.

It was not until 1886 that positive findings and therefore answers to the Silbury mysteries were uncovered. In that year, the amateur archaeologist Alfred Pass investigated Silbury's enormous ditch. Generally around 40m wide to the south, east and northern sides of the mound, the ditch extends to around 140m to the west. Pass discovered the mound must pre-date not only the Roman period, but also the Iron and Bronze Ages.

He sank a series of shafts into the ditch down to the natural solid chalk, which yielded depths of between 4.5m to 6.5m of silting. In one situated close to the mound where the shafts were generally around 6.5m deep, a Roman coin was found at a depth of almost 2m. That was a clear indication that only the upper third of the ditch deposits had accumulated since the Roman period. In another shaft, at a depth of around 3m, the ditch deposits contained a 3 centimetres layer of black material. A human femur and numerous flint flakes were found in the layer. This led Pass to comment that the monument was "erected by a people...so little advanced in civilisation, that they were using flint implements a long time after the hill was built".

Pass had placed Silbury conclusively in the Stone Age; a period without grave goods of any monetary value, and almost certainly without kings. He duly published his groundbreaking findings, yet over 80 years later when Silbury was being prepared for the most comprehensive investigation in its history, the excavator Professor Richard Atkinson said he expected to find the mound belonged to the Bronze Age. In 1968, Atkinson attempted to capitalise on the work of Alfred Pass, but since then, the ditch that Pass had clearly demonstrated to be a repository of chronologically accurate deposits has been largely ignored!

The next significant event in Silbury's history occurred in 1873 when the estate containing the mound was put up for auction. Sir

John Lubbock purchased it, and promptly placed it within the guardianship of the Ancient Monuments Board. At last, the monument was no longer vulnerable to the whim of private owners.

In 1922, the famous Egyptologist Flinders Petrie became interested in Silbury, probably because of its pyramidal form. He excavated two trenches on the lower slope of the mound adjacent to the eastern causeway, in the entirely reasonable hope of finding an entrance or a chamber in a sunrise-orientated location. No such features were discovered, although Petrie found the old land surface in that sector either had been completely stripped of turf and topsoil prior to the building of the mound, or that the ground level had been lowered. He also found that the eastern causeway consisted of solid chalk covered with chalk rubble to form a smooth gradient.

The first investigation of the relatively modern era took place in 1959 when F. R. McKim conducted an electrical resistivity survey of the entire mound. His equipment should have detected any inner chambers or passageways, but nothing was found. In those days the technique was in its infancy, and conveniently for all king-hunters, the results were deemed inconclusive.

1968. Atkinson and the BBC.

Professor Richard Atkinson was approached by the BBC in the 1960s with a proposal to re-open Silbury. Archaeology had proven popular with television viewers in the early years of the corporation, and because of Atkinson's previous high-profile excavations at Stonehenge he was undoubtedly the most popular archaeologist of the time. An ambitious project was carefully planned throughout 1966/67 as excitement grew within the BBC and the archaeological community.

Possibly with the BBC's budget in his thoughts, Atkinson whetted the public and corporate appetites by repeating the tradition that a horse and king "the size of life and of solid gold" might be buried within the mound, and even suggested that it could be the tomb of Stonehenge's architect. Why the architect of a relatively small monument located sixteen miles from Silbury should be honoured by interment in the greatest of all mounds less than one mile from the enormous Avebury henge, Atkinson did not make clear. In a more realistic vein he stated, "The most likely hypothesis is that it is a burial mound of exceptional size", and he insisted the principal purpose of the investigation was to establish the composition and date of the mound. He believed the site to be unique and that it would yield insights into the "social and political structure of the society which encompassed it." The BBC's provision for five-minute programmes every day "over the crucial period" implied a somewhat less realistic attitude on their part.

It was decided that the least damaging and most economical way to access the interior of the mound was by way of the 1849 tunnel. There had been a number of roof falls within the tunnel over the years owing to the lack of backfilling, and a new entrance had to be created. This was slightly higher and to the east of the 1849 entrance, and was designed to intersect the old tunnel around 20m inside the mound.

Tunnelling began in April 1968, carried out by staff and students of the Mining Department of Cardiff University under the supervision of Dr John Taylor and coal miner Bill Curtis. In early July, they broke through into the 1849 tunnel only to find that the old roof had collapsed almost along its full length, rendering progress slow and difficult. Initially, Atkinson and his colleagues had to crawl into the tunnel and then scramble over piles of rubble, but that did not detract from what Atkinson described as a "fantastic experience." Evidently, he was quite stunned by the variety of materials he found within the mound, first discovering chalk blocks in the tunnel walls, then the organic materials at the centre which he described as a "highly coloured layer cake".

The tunnel was cleared of rubble, and steel arches were inserted to make it safe. As the tunnel was being cleared, Atkinson discovered a buried ditch that had been cut into the old ground surface, and it was this that allowed him to postulate the three main stages of construction of the mound that remain pretty much accepted to this day. These will be described in much greater detail later, for subsequent investigations have refined our knowledge of the site, but Atkinson's proposed sequence can be summarised as follows.

Silbury Hill's construction began when a small mound of dull, golden gravel was deposited on an almost level section at the centre of a generally sloping chalk promontory. The small gravel mound was then covered by a mound of turf and topsoil. In turn, this was covered by four layers of black marshy soil, white chalk and coloured flint gravel. The height of this mound had to be estimated at around 5m because the tunnel was not high enough to uncover the top of it. Later, when repairs were carried out to sections of the tunnel that needed new arches, Atkinson extended the old Merewether lateral tunnels, and found the organic deposits had an overall diameter of around 34m. Atkinson labelled this Silbury I. The state of preservation of this central core was astonishing, and when a piece of turf was removed it was found still to be green, with both plant and insect remains looking like they had been placed there the day before. Ants' wings found in the turves infamously led to the conclusion that the central core must have been constructed in August of whichever year, as ants only have wings at that time of year. Although that is true, subsequent research has proven the August construction theory to be unsound because the turves had almost certainly been stockpiled.

Silbury II consisted of chalk that had been extracted from the buried ditch and then piled on top of Silbury I. Atkinson believed that Silbury II was conical in form, and found that it had a diameter of around 73m. He also investigated the buried ditch and found that its sides appeared to be unweathered, which led him to surmise that Silbury II must have been covered very soon after its construction. Therefore, a short time after completion of Silbury II, the builders had excavated chalk from a new outer ditch (Silbury's present surrounding ditch). This material was used to backfill the inner ditch, and then both the ditch and Silbury II were covered by more chalk from the enormous outer ditch to form Silbury III. With its flat top at an average height of 31m above the top of the promontory, and with a diameter around 167m, this is the mound we see today (figures 1 and 2).

Figure 1 is effectively a plan of Silbury's contents. Figure 2 shows the extent of slippage of surface material from the mound that has widened its base, and the depth of silting that has filled the outer ditch.

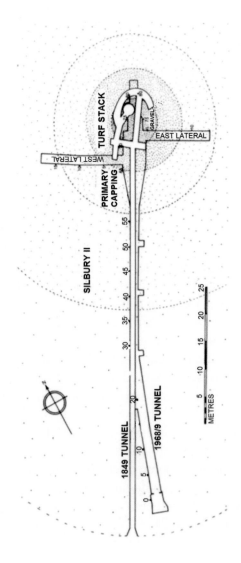

Figure 1. After Whittle.

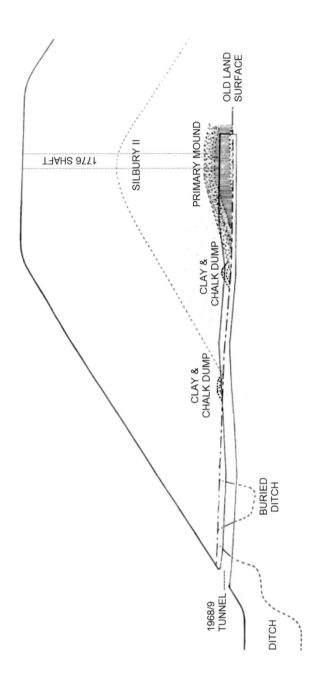

Figure 2. After Whittle.

All that may lead the reader to conclude that construction of the mound was quite a crude undertaking, with piles of material simply overlying each other. However, as Atkinson was to discover, there is much more to Silbury Hill than that. It is in fact a masterpiece of engineering, devised and constructed by people with a comprehensive understanding of soil mechanics.

Atkinson did not limit his investigation merely to tunnelling. Trenches were cut on the slopes and the summit of the mound, and boreholes drilled down to the old ground surface. Also, new techniques in surveying provided contour plans, geophysics and seismic analysis. From all these he amassed evidence of the stepped pyramidal form of Silbury III that had previously been undetected and totally unsuspected.

Each of Atkinson's proposed six steps appeared to be around 5m high and formed by horizontal layers of chalk rubble contained within radial and concentric chalk walls (picture a spider's web covering a wedding cake). Clearly, the builders had gone to great lengths to ensure stability of Silbury III and therefore longevity of the mound. If they had not done so, then Silbury could not possibly have survived in anything like its present form. The completed steps of the 'cake' were then packed or 'iced' with chalk rubble taken from the western extension of the outer ditch to produce the smooth and conical appearance of the mound. It was this purely cosmetic undertaking that Atkinson came to label as Silbury IV, although it is in effect simply the finishing touch of Silbury III.

To this day, there is still part of a sloping 'terrace' clearly visible just below the summit, and similar anomalies further down the slopes. Atkinson's trenches uncovered evidence that the upper terrace is probably of Neolithic construction, defined as it is on the inside by a wall of chalk blocks. The terrace was found to have been polished smooth, presumably by the feet of workers carrying chalk rubble. Thus, Atkinson had uncovered the very first evidence of a Neolithic spiral walkway on Silbury Hill. Atkinson suspected that although of Neolithic origin, the terrace had been modified at a much later period, probably in Saxon times.

Further insights were gained by borings in the northern sector of the outer ditch, which indicated a maximum depth of 9m of silting.

Intriguingly, the ditch deposits were studied by Barbara Hart-Jones, who concluded that the ditch must have been water-filled in the past owing to the number of water snails within it. Atkinson disagreed because he could not envisage any circumstances in which the ditch could have been dug if the ground was wet – but much more on that later. A section cut across the southern ditch between the two causeways uncovered a depth of 10m of silting, and found that the outer face of the ditch rises almost vertically to a point where it underlies the modern road. A series of steps consisting of clay and chalk protected by a wooden revetment were found on the base of the mound itself; further proof that the builders had taken great care to protect their monument from weathering.

Work continued until the autumn of 1969. Atkinson returned in 1970 to complete his work on the summit, discovering a series of four concentric walls of chalk blocks that held the mound's horizontally-laid chalk rubble in place. He had plans for further extensive investigations, but the BBC's patience had run out along with their budget. They had hoped to give their viewers sensational treasures, and they believed they had failed to do so. It did not appear to have occurred to them that Atkinson's discovery of Silbury's stepped pyramidal structure was sensational in itself. Finally, with only the tunnel backfilled and the central void and lateral tunnels left open, a steel door at the entrance was closed and the investigation was over. Radiocarbon dating was very much in its infancy at the time, although the results indicated initial construction sometime between 2871 and 2486 BC, and for many years the figure 2660 BC was generally accepted.

So, after one of the most innovative and remarkable archaeological interventions in history, Silbury had proven to be a more perplexing mystery than anyone had imagined. Atkinson never completed his report of the investigation. Perhaps we should not be surprised about that, because although he had previously published a book on his excavations at Stonehenge, the great bulk of his field notes about that site remained firmly in his head and accompanied him to his grave in 1994. It was not until 1997 that Atkinson's work on Silbury was properly written up by Alasdair Whittle for his book *Sacred Mound, Holy Rings* (Oxbow 1997).

May 2000. The Inevitable Calamity.

It was only a matter of time before inadequate backfilling of all the archaeological excavations caused major problems to the mound. Sure enough, after a period of excessive rainfall in May 2000, a hole appeared on the top of Silbury Hill. Initially measuring about 2.5m square and around 13m deep, it was obviously the shaft that had been excavated in 1776. It transpired that instead of backfilling the shaft, the miners had simply fitted a wooden platform near the top and covered that instead. Inevitably, the platform rotted and collapsed. Subsequently, aerial photographs taken in the 1930s were re-examined and shown to demonstrate that a slump in the shaft had been present in that era, and that the infill must have been topped up from time to time.

The archaeological establishment was on full alert, with English Heritage Inspectors and structural engineers swarming all over the mound, and an aerial survey team monitoring the situation. Security fencing was swiftly erected to protect both the shaft and the public, although the authorities' appeals for the public to stay away from a 13m window into Neolithic building practices were clearly going to fall on deaf ears. To further protect the exposed shaft, a cover of corrugated tin sheeting with a door for inspection purposes was fitted above the hole. Archaeologists were lowered in harnesses to record the clearly visible layers in the shaft sides, and to take samples for environmental analysis. They were not the only ones excited at the prospect of seeing the inside of one of the world's most intriguing monuments, and soon a video of the interior was being touted on the internet by the Dutch authors Bert Janssen and Janet Ossebard.

They had acquired the video from two people who were believed to live locally (they did indeed; I met one of them). Those two people had unwittingly risked their lives in an act that demonstrated complete disregard for the very monument they claimed to revere. Not once but twice, they had abseiled down the shaft and trampled around on the collapsed material within (something the archaeologists had taken great care not to do). The pair clearly had not realised there were almost certainly further voids below their feet that could swallow them up at any given moment, and trigger further collapses in the shaft sides *above their heads*. While it can never be proven, it is very likely that it was these two people who caused the damage to the shaft that very soon resulted in a further collapse at the top of the hole, extending the surface void from 2.5m square to 5m by 7m, and destroying irreplaceable archaeological deposits. The eminent archaeologist Mike Pitts wrote at the time, "The level of their idiocy boggles the mind".

Meanwhile, the Dutch video and other internet sites proclaimed that English Heritage were keeping quiet about the existence of 'secret' tunnels in the mound, which actually were voids caused by the upward migration of collapsing archaeological excavations. As it transpired, the two abseilers were not the only trespassers, and staff from English Heritage and the National Trust were kept busy removing other sightseers. Around the time of the Winter Solstice, a group of people were observed in Avebury's Red Lion pub handing out pieces of sarsen stones they had removed from the bottom of the hole, which by that time was only 4m deep having been partially infilled by further collapses. I didn't know it at the time, but it now seems very likely that I saw the same group of people on the day they defiled Silbury.

There were three of them, one female and two males. I was watching them from Waden Hill, and I could not believe my eyes. Not only did they climb over the fence around the collapsed summit platform, they actually tore off at least one of the fence signs that implored people to keep out of the damaged area and respect the monument. Then it got far worse. Before leaping down into the hole, they stamped heavily around its perimeter, deliberately trying to dislodge even more material! Once inside the hole, they proceeded to throw material out of it, any scrap of which could have contained vital radiocarbon-dating evidence. By the time I reached Silbury they had already left. Later, I read an account of people handing out sarsen fragments in the pub, and the dates coincided.

The authorities could not have known it at the time, but however disturbing to them the collapsing monument and public interference may have been, all that was nothing compared to the predicament they were about to find themselves in. Having believed the solution to the problem would simply entail the infilling of the collapsed shaft with some suitable material, it soon became evident that the state of the mound was much more perilous. Additional voids within its structure were being detected by seismic survey, and even more were suspected.

The possibility that Silbury Hill was actually in danger of irreversible and total collapse had to be seriously considered. I remember how grateful I was that the nightmare situation was not my problem. Of course I was deeply concerned, as was everyone else with a respect for our prehistoric heritage, but can you even begin to imagine how the authorities felt about the imminent loss of such a renowned monument *on their watch?* What a way to go down in history! Eventually they did prevail, although it would be fully eight years before the final repairs were made and everyone could enjoy a collective sigh of relief. How they did it will be described later.

It was during English Heritage's great dilemma that I began my own field research into Silbury Hill, hoping that the great mound would still exist in a recognisable form once I had finished.

Part 3. The theories.

In 2001, our knowledge of Silbury Hill could be summarised as follows: at some time in the Late Neolithic period *c.*2600 BC, a highly motivated people had constructed Europe's largest monumental mound on a natural promontory situated in the basin of the Upper Kennet Valley. At the core of the massive pyramidal structure was a primary mound of gravel overlain by vegetable matter, which was then covered by layers of mixed earth, gravel and soil. The next stage consisted of a conical mound of chalk rubble, which was in turn covered by an extremely skilfully engineered third stage utilising radial and concentric chalk walls infilled with chalk rubble. The chalk of this third stage had been quarried from the mound's surrounding ditch that had completely silted up over thousands of years.

Including the height of its natural promontory base, the final monument stood 37m tall, and would have towered up to 47m above the bottom of the ditch at the time of construction. Roughly conical in shape, the mound had a flat top about 28m in diameter, a base diameter of around 167m and occupied over 5 acres. Despite extensive archaeological investigations, no chambers of any kind had been detected and were not expected to be.

What were we to make of all this? Silbury Hill was unquestionably the most enigmatic Neolithic monument in Europe. It was not the business of archaeologists to speculate, and predictably they were relatively silent on the matter, although Alasdair Whittle had suggested the mound was a metaphor for the Earth itself. In addition, the periodical *Antiquity* (volume 65, 1991, pp 894-8) had published an article by Paul Devereux in which he had made some fascinating landscape observations, disproving along the way the "frequently repeated fallacy" (ibid) that Silbury cannot be seen from within Avebury henge. Many years after publication of Devereux's article, some archaeologists still fervently denied the intervisibility of the sites, simply because the official English Heritage book about Avebury's monuments did so.

In 2003, I experienced another example of the stubbornness of some of those within the archaeological community. Back in 1995, together with many colleagues, Dr. Rosemund Cleal (curator of Avebury's Alexander Keiller Museum) collated all published and unpublished data that had ever been written about Stonehenge, and provided a critical list of radiocarbon assays. Their book *Stonehenge in its Landscape* (English Heritage Archaeological Report 10. 1995) became the definitive publication on the monument with regard to archaeological data.

They proved that Stonehenge's sarsen circle and trilithon horseshoe were constructed *c.*2500 BC, and that the earliest phase dated back a further 500 years. That was 500 to 1,000 years older than previously thought for all phases, depending on which 'authority' one had previously believed, and conclusively dated the monument to the Late Stone Age. That always should have been obvious; Stonehenge must represent a monument constructed towards the end of an era, otherwise it would not be one of a kind. Fully eight years after publication of the book, I was at Stonehenge when I heard a National Trust/English Heritage tour guide telling a party of American visitors that the sarsen circle and horseshoe were Bronze Age and could not have been erected before 2100 BC. Later, in a quiet aside with the tour guide when I respectfully pointed out his mistake and the source of my information, it was obvious that he considered the 1995 publication to be a modern irrelevance. I don't know how much the National Trust charged their party of visitors for the privilege of being so misinformed.

Getting back to the earlier point, Paul Devereux wrote that from within a structure inside Avebury henge known as the Z-feature, the summit platform and the upper 'ledge' of Silbury are visible above the intervening ground of Waden Hill, with the effect that the distant horizon beyond Silbury appears to emanate from that section of the mound. He discovered the relationship between Silbury and the distant horizon was evident from the East Kennet, West Kennet and Beckhampton long barrows and the Sanctuary circle. "In each case, the skyline can be seen visually to intersect the Silbury profile between the platform-like summit and the ledge" (ibid). Although there are many more monuments within the Avebury complex, especially long barrows, from which the horizon does not intersect with Silbury in that way, Devereux's investigation and findings were refreshingly innovative.

He also proposed a 'double sunrise' effect, whereby standing first on Silbury's summit and then by descending to the ledge, an observer would witness two sunrises. Firstly, above the distant horizon, and secondly above nearby Waden Hill, which would form part of the skyline when viewed from the lower aspect of the ledge. The section of the skyline formed by Waden Hill would align with the sunrises of the Celtic festivals of Beltane and Lughnasa in early May and August. Nevertheless, if one was to stand on *any* hill facing two very closely aligned ridges, the same thing could be made to happen. By watching the initial sunrise and then descending to a point where the closer ridge formed part of the horizon, another 'double sunrise' would occur. It would not be necessary to build a hill to see this, and it certainly could not be sufficient motivation to build the colossal Silbury mound (not that Devereux actually claimed that it was).

His proposal leant very heavily on the implication that the ledge was a designated viewing area, whereas it had been found by Atkinson's excavations to be part of a medieval fortification that had utilised a section of a spirally constructed Neolithic walkway. If not a walkway, the ledge would be evidence that the entire frame of Silbury III had been constructed spirally, and in either case the ledge could not be a separate Neolithic feature. Devereux made clear that his topographical and astronomical proposals, if true, would only have been components in a much "broader conceptual scheme", and that they would not have "excluded other factors of perceived religious significance associated with the site by the monument's builders" (ibid).

On a similar theme, although much more esoteric, the renowned dowsers Hamish Miller and Paul Broadhurst wrote of Silbury Hill in *The Sun and The Serpent* (Pendragon Press 1989). Directed by Brian Ashley, the owner of the Avebury henge shop, they located 'earth energy spirals' on Knoll Down, which they believed to be the terminus of Beckhampton's long-lost avenue of standing stones. No matter how unconventional such ideas may be, I am not subject to the professional constraints of archaeology, and for myself *any* proposal is worthy of consideration until found to be otherwise. After all, dowsing has proved to be an effective method of locating underground water, and is even practised in oil and mineral exploration. If earth energies really exist, dowsing could be a way to detect them. Personal experience under the tutelage of Avebury's leading dowser Maria Wheatley leads me to believe there really is something in it, although I do not believe that anyone fully understands the phenomenon.

From the location of Miller and Broadhurst's proposed energy spiral, it is possible to find gaps in the trees on Knoll Down in order to look eastward at Silbury Hill and beyond to the site of the Sanctuary stone circle. The Sanctuary site appears to sit directly on Silbury's flat top, and marks the terminus of the West Kennet Avenue. From the Sanctuary, of course, the sightline is reversed and Knoll Down 'crowns' Silbury. For Miller and Broadhurst, this was evidence that Silbury was a communications centre; a platform from which the termini of both the West Kennet and Beckhampton Avenues could be observed, allowing religious processions to be co-ordinated to arrive at the henge simultaneously. Their landscape observations clearly are accurate, but there is no archaeological evidence that the Beckhampton Avenue carried on as far as Knoll Down. In the 18th century, William Stukeley saw parts of the avenue that no longer exist, and he claimed it actually ended to the south of Knoll Down at Fox Covert.

Miller and Broadhurst arrived in Avebury on a quest to track an earth energy current known as the 'St. Michael Line', which is said to run from the western tip of Cornwall to the extreme eastern part of East Anglia. On their journey, they claim to have discovered that the Michael current interweaves with a female current, which they christened 'The Mary Line.' According to Miller and Broadhurst, the Mary Line runs through Avebury henge alongside the Michael Line, then departs to run southwards through Silbury Hill. However, they did not claim the female current had anything to do with Silbury's location or form.

In 1976, Michael Dames produced a work that became the classic romantic interpretation of Silbury Hill: *The Silbury Treasure – The Great Goddess Rediscovered* (Thames and Hudson 1976).

Although not universally accepted, and certainly not by mainstream archaeology, there is a widely held belief that the pre-eminent deity of the Stone Age was the Great Goddess or Earth Mother. Dames asserted that Silbury is a metaphor for the Earth, and as previously stated, the eminent archaeologist Alasdair Whittle has supported this view. Dames believes the mound *and* ditch are in fact an earth sculpture, the plan of which represents the body of the Goddess in human form (figure 3).

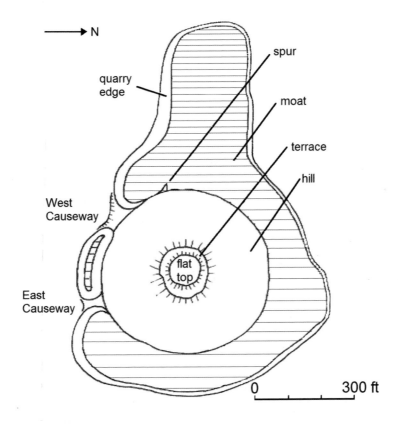

Figure 3. After Dames.

For Dames, the great mound itself represents the pregnant Earth Mother about to give birth at harvest time. The irregularly shaped ditch, in profile, and when viewed from the summit platform, depicts the head, back, vulva and knee of the Goddess, while the short ditch between the causeways is a symbol of the new-born child or "baby-grain". Also, there is an outcrop of the natural spur on which the mound is built that is hidden beneath the silt in the ditch. This was discovered during the Atkinson investigations in one of a series of borings. Dames believes the hidden outcrop delineates the breast of the Goddess figure, and it certainly would be located correctly to do so. The Goddess was bestowed with human characteristics because for the Neolithic people "the cyclical order of nature was mirrored by human experience" (ibid). Thus, human fertility was interwoven with the Earth's bounty.

Of course, all this requires a great leap of faith, especially in view of the fact that Dames's Goddess figure cannot be seen in full from any one particular point: a bird's-eye view or at least a strong imagination would be necessary. Nevertheless, if I may contribute something to his theory, the three main stages of construction of the mound are suggestive of the tripartite nature of the Goddess, often described as Maiden, Mother and Crone. The Maiden could be represented by the primary organic deposits kept eternally fresh in the airless conditions at the heart of the mound (at least until the archaeologists got there). The chalk mound of stage two could symbolise the transition to motherhood, and it will become evident later in these pages why the final stage could represent the all-seeing eye and wisdom of the Crone.

It wasn't until around 2001 that attitudes regarding Silbury's ditch began to change. Prior to that, most archaeologists believed that during the Late Neolithic the ditch would have remained dry. Dames insisted that the ditch was designed to hold water, a view with which I have always concurred. Where better than the valley basin to dig down into the water-table? In wet winter months the silted ditch sometimes still floods. This will be discussed in much greater detail later, but at the time of my initial research the 'dry ditch' doctrine was very controversial. The importance of water to Silbury Hill's Neolithic environment was obvious to anyone with a rudimentary understanding of the area's hydrology, and the archaeological community's intransigence on the matter was very puzzling.

Either ingeniously or imaginatively, Dames plotted the course of the sun and moon's reflections on the hypothetical water surface. He described the heavenly bodies combining with the vulva, baby and breast of the monument at appropriate times of year. The intention was to "correlate solar and lunar events to fertilise the Earth symbol" (ibid). All that may seem too good to be true, but it is a breathtakingly beautiful concept nevertheless. In its defence, I would say that conventional religions with all their intangible deities are relatively modern inventions, and that Neolithic belief systems would have been much more strongly influenced by the observation of nature. The natural world's deities could be seen and their powers actually experienced at first hand. Also, deliberate alignment on solar or lunar events, and focus on shafts of sunlight and moonlight is definitely in evidence at other Neolithic monuments. The intention could very well have been to create a symbolic act of fertilisation, which would have been the result of harmonizing the Earth with the sun and moon within those monuments. It could be argued that the principal function of many Neolithic monuments, and stone circles in particular, was to embody that harmony.

A prime example of this can be found in the stone setting known as 'The Cove' within Avebury henge. Of the original three stones, only the backstone and one of its flanking stones are still in place. The backstone is known to be around 100 tonnes in weight, probably making it the heaviest megalith in Britain. It leans at a quite alarming angle, and when an attempt was made to right it, the archaeological team abandoned their effort to uncover the base of the stone after they had reached a depth of 1.1m below the natural chalk surface. They estimated that the stone socket continued to a depth of 1.5m below the chalk line, which is a total of 3m (10ft) below the modern surface that conceals an accumulation of rubbish dating from the medieval period up to the 20th century. The estimated depth of 1.5m for the original socket is exceptional when compared with the average depth of 0.6m of other excavated stones in the henge. Another peculiarity of the backstone was the presence of compartmentalised areas in the materials used to pack its socket. "Such 'staged' filling might have allowed the stone to be temporarily supported while still capable of being manipulated into its correct position" (Gillings & Pollard, *Avebury,* Duckworth 2004). Nevertheless, it was concluded that the stone had been lowered into the hole where it rested at an angle, and then proved too difficult for the Neolithic people to pull upright. On the other hand, if I wanted such a heavy stone to lean, I know I would have to insert it into an unusually deep hole, and that it would require extra manipulation. It leans in a most significant direction, and its flanking stone points exactly the same way.

The Cove is almost certainly one of the oldest stone settings in the henge, dating to around 3000 BC. Within this simple triple-stone arrangement, the builders managed to embody the harmony between the Earth, sun and moon quite ingeniously. In the Late Neolithic, anyone standing inside the Cove would have seen only two close horizons within the observable range of sunsets. These are formed by Windmill Hill and Folly Hill. The Summer Solstice sun would have been seen to set directly in the centre of Windmill Hill's causewayed enclosures, and the Winter Solstice sun to set in the centre of Folly Hill, which Julian Cope describes as "the great lost sacred eminence of this landscape" (*The Modern Antiquarian,* Thorsons 1998). Although there only remains a small tumulus on the hill, it appears to have had considerable earthworks around the modern road that now cuts right through it.

Therefore, the Cove is located where the sacred landscape is seen to combine with the solstitial sunsets, but its actual alignment is with the Northern Major rising of the moon. The backstone is set at right angles to the moon and leans towards it, while the clearly defined long axis of the remaining flanking stone points straight at the serene, gleaming orb. That was perfectly evident in December 2006 when the event was witnessed by only myself and three other people! That experience bonds the four of us forever. Three of us also were at Callanish in the Western Isles that year for the moon's Southern Major rising.

In 1998, the musician and poet Julian Cope produced his magnificent tome *The Modern Antiquarian*. He absolutely has no doubt that Silbury is an Earth Goddess figure, and his book conducts the reader on a fascinating pilgrimage throughout Britain's

**Picture 2. The Avebury Cove. Ten feet of the leaning backstone
is below ground.**

'Bridget landscapes'. According to Cope, 'Bridget' and 'Bride' are just two of an entire lexicon of names by which the Goddess was known. It seems highly likely that the names were the origin of many place-names throughout these islands, and probably of Britain's name itself. Although I will be making many more references to his book later, I could never hope to do justice to his work by attempting any précis, so do yourself a favour and buy it!

In 1902, Moses Cotsworth claimed that Silbury had supported a 29m-tall post for casting a shadow onto the flat land below, upon which a giant sundial had been laid out. Presumably, he was unaware that in the Late Neolithic there wasn't any flat land below, only the ditch. In *Prehistoric Avebury* (Yale University Press 2002), the archaeologist and prolific writer Aubrey Burl had effectively demolished Cotsworth's theory, and went on to propose that the inspiration for Silbury's construction may be found in Yorkshire, specifically in the large round barrows of Duggleby Howe, Wold Newton and Willy Howe. Large as they undoubtedly are, or at least once were, the tallest of them was only around 9m high, and there are larger mounds and natural cone-shaped hills very much closer to Silbury than Yorkshire.

In 2002, the inevitable UFO theory was offered up by John Cowie in his *Silbury Dawning: The Alien Visitor Gene Theory*, in which we were informed that Silbury was built 13,000 years ago by benign extraterrestrials who shared not only their great wisdom with the ancient Britons, but also their genes. That would be the greatest story ever told if there was any truth in it. Unfortunately, all the archaeological evidence indicates there is none whatsoever. I had to open a new file for that one, where it was joined three years later by Lothar Respondek's *The Mystery of Silbury Hill* (Elar 2005). The book contains some very impressive and comprehensive research into environmental records, and it was obvious the author had read Whittle's account of Atkinson's excavations; he republished some of the diagrams and included the book in his bibliography. He must have been fully aware of the complexity of Silbury's construction and the immense effort of its builders to ensure longevity of the mound. Nevertheless, he claimed this exceptional piece of Neolithic engineering was primarily a spoil heap, and that the builders' main intention was to dig a deep ditch for use as a well during a period of drought. He also appeared to have missed the fact that Silbury's earliest ditches were on the top of a promontory, where nobody would think of digging a well.

Part 4. The landscape shapes an idea.

Around 2001, the aforementioned theories just about amounted to the sum total of attempts to rationalise the Silbury enigma. It wasn't much to work with, and I was becoming convinced that archaeology could never offer a satisfactory solution. I was surprised to find myself leaning towards the Earth Mother school of thought, but that seemed to be emerging as the most logical approach. Also, I did not entirely trust archaeological interpretations of Neolithic monuments, particularly those relating to long barrows, most of which are believed to pre-date Silbury by around a thousand years. Unless there had been a cataclysmic upheaval in ethnic population and culture in the intervening period, the long barrows should provide a window into the past, and enlighten us as to the religious traditions from which Silbury evolved. On that particular point, it is important to bear in mind that Silbury is Neolithic and does not belong to the later Bronze Age when burial rites did indeed change, and the tradition of communal interments in long barrows became individual burials in round barrows. The absence of any burial or chamber, and its unique location in a valley basin proves that Silbury is not a round barrow, although subsequently it may have become the inspiration for some of them.

One of the most deeply entrenched tenets of British archaeology is the purely funereal function of long barrows and other megalithic 'tombs'. Relatively few complete burials have been found in the chambers of long barrows, although masses of disarticulated and wildly disordered bones are common. In many cases only one bone from individual burials has been discovered, mixed with the bones of others. In some long barrows there were no human bones whatsoever. The great megalithic domes of Newgrange in Ireland and Maes Howe in Orkney were found to be practically empty. Yet with very few exceptions, in academic texts those domes and all long barrows are described as tombs.

There is an episode of Channel 4's *Time Team* in which a local expert conducts a member of the team around Maes Howe. Having expounded the virtues of the "tomb", the expert concludes, "All that is missing are the burials." I stand to be corrected on this, but it seems to me that burials are prerequisite components of tombs, and complete burials at that.

Tests have found that many bones exhumed from long barrows carry signs of disease, and that all the unfortunate occupants died at a relatively early age to modern standards. At Avebury's renowned West Kennet long barrow for example, the deceased comprised of a foetus, infants, children, one youth and upwards of twenty adults. The eldest is believed to have died in his forties, possibly killed by an arrow. Where are the older people? Are we to accept the standard view that Neolithic people were a sickly, short-lived lot? In a personal communication with Dr. Rosemund Cleal I was informed "from prehistoric burial populations in general there is quite a lot of evidence particularly for poor nutrition caused either by lack of food at some times or the prevalence of diseases such as gastro-enteritis. At least one human bone specialist I know is convinced that poor health caused by cooking and eating utensils being contaminated more or less all the time was widespread."

For such a supposedly hard-pressed people, the monuments they built attest to bags of energy, strength and steely determination. That would appear to be evidence of a healthy population, and it is written in stone throughout our Neolithic landscapes. In an age without tobacco, air pollution, pesticides or any chemicals in food, and in which most people would have enjoyed healthy outdoor lifestyles, surely at least some would have lived long lives.

Neolithic cremations are widespread and numerous throughout Britain, and many are contemporary with the period of long barrow usage. Something must have set apart the vast majority of the dead who were cremated or excarnated from the few who had at least some part of their remains placed in the long barrows. It is not unreasonable to propose that the common thread linking long barrow interments, and the reason those people seem to have been set apart, *is* the fact they died young or before their time, either by illness, accident or misadventure. This would suggest untimely death was anathema to people who lived closely with the rhythms of nature, and that anything breaking the cyclical order would have to be redressed.

A reportedly 'enigmatic' feature of long barrows is the excessive length of the mounds compared to the brevity of their chambered areas. At West Kennet, the chambers occupy only around one tenth of the mound's total length. A possible solution to the mystery can be found in the restricted womb and extended torso-like characteristics of long barrows, which are there for all to see. Archaeological investigations have demonstrated that rituals took place at the temple/barrow, which involved the destruction and then rebuilding of the forecourt. Nobody has described these rituals more eloquently or graphically than Julian Cope: "This was symbolic of the vagina's destruction in childbirth...And in returning the dead to a foetal position, in the womb-like megalithic chambers, so the soul was prepared for its journey of rebirth" (ibid). It is conceivable that selected remains of the chosen few were placed into the Earth Mother's womb chambers in the expectation or hope they would be reborn, and thus be given another chance to complete their life cycles. That would provide some comfort to the bereaved, and there are echoes of such hopes and beliefs in modern religions, funeral rites and Biblical events.

Of course, all that is highly speculative, but it is every bit as valid as the conventional model. My point being that archaeology's 'axioms' are in fact questionable. One outstanding exception to the academic norm is Miles Russell's *Monuments of the British Neolithic* (Tempus 2002). He points out that even the 'flagship' barrows of the sepulchral school of thought, where large quantities of human bones have been found, "seem to relate to structures demolished prior to the building of the mound itself " (ibid).

Russell argues that long barrows were in fact communal archives, which explains the deposits of human and animal bones with artefacts such as pottery. The very material from which they were constructed also indicates a desire to build an archive. That is especially true of the West Kennet long barrow near Silbury Hill, which does not consist only of chalk taken from the ditches running along its flanks, but also includes materials selected from various other locations in the barrow's wider environs. "Evidence for the deposition of articulated, disassembled, disarticulated or cremated human bone within linear mounds may have little to do with burial in the conventional sense" (Russell, ibid).

The long barrow builders were the ancestors of the people who would come to build Silbury Hill, and it could have been the beliefs and traditions of those ancestors that provided the inspiration and purpose for the great mound. Far too many academic writers have dismissed the Earth Mother or Goddess religion as a myth: evidence for it is all around us in both monuments and landscapes, and it was inevitable that Silbury's landscape should become the principal focus for my research. It could never have been Silbury's archaeological record because that was leading nowhere, and to this day that situation has not changed.

The long barrow-shaped eminence of Waden Hill rises just a stone's throw away from Silbury, and practically adjoins Avebury henge. It wasn't long before a relationship between Waden Hill and the area's long barrows became evident. It appeared, with only one exception, that the valley's long barrows west of the natural boundary of the Ridgeway were located and built to such a height that an observer standing on the barrow mound would see at least the summit of Waden Hill, and vice-versa. The exception is Roughridge Hill long barrow, but I believe it was considered by the local Neolithic people to belong to a quite separate cluster of barrows that are located on or near the escarpment forming the Avebury region's southern boundary. That places them outside of Waden Hill's territory, and none of those barrows are visible from Waden Hill.

The best-preserved barrow of the southern cluster is Adam's Grave, which unlike most long barrows is not long and flat, but rises to a pinnacle at one end. A report written by Sir Richard Colt Hoare in 1821 states "the ridge of this tumulus is more acute than any I have seen." All the long barrows in the Adam's Grave cluster are intervisible with Etchilhampton Hill near Devizes, which has an acute ridge and rises to a pinnacle at one end.

Over to the east of the Ridgeway, I suspect that Rockley Down served the same purpose as Waden and Etchilhampton Hills. West of Waden's territory, another hill somewhere in the Calne/Chippenham area could have served King's Play long barrow. There are insufficient points of reference to know exactly which hill, although there are a number of suitably shaped candidates. That would make four mother landmark hills in the region. One of those four natural landmarks is visible from every positively identified long barrow, and crucially at every site it *is* only one of them. I think that was a deliberate arrangement.

Were long barrows built in the image of their mother landmark? I believe they were, although there are simply too many sites that have been loosely identified as long barrows to be certain. Also, there is the question of 'Dolmens' such as Devil's Den, which may or may not be the remains of long barrows. My guess is they were not (Miles Russell agrees), but only archaeological investigation can prove it. Whatever, at the early stages of my fieldwork, I thought there was a strong likelihood of a pre-Silbury tradition of landmark or mother hills from which sightlines were an important factor. I fully expected to find that sightlines from or to the great artificial hill also would have a territorial function of some kind.

Part 5. In the field.

The view from Silbury Hill.

The next step was to compare the view from Silbury with those from other high vantage points in the area to ascertain if there are any significant differences. It was no easy task: my fieldwork ran head-on into the Foot and Mouth crisis, and English Heritage had declared Silbury totally out of bounds with absolutely no exceptions other than their own staff. Amanda Chadburn, the Inspector of Ancient Monuments, kindly came to the rescue by taking pictures of the complete horizon visible from Silbury's summit. I had at least something to work with, although it wasn't until I studied maps of the area that I began to see something of possible significance in Silbury's location and height.

Our archaeological knowledge of Silbury has improved since the 2007 work to stabilise the great mound, although at the time of my field research our knowledge did not go beyond anything later than the Atkinson excavations of 1968. As previously stated, evidence gathered from Atkinson's work indicated that Silbury's third stage of construction involved a stepped pyramidal structure. Close to the top is the clearly visible 'terrace' that Atkinson believed to be an original although later modified feature. A recent survey by English Heritage uncovered evidence the mound may actually have been constructed spirally, or that a spiral walkway was cut into it. That indicates the terrace is simply an upper section of the original spiral form or walkway, extant mainly because it would not have been subject to the same amount of slippage and covering as the lower sections. Atkinson himself had mentioned the possibility of this. Spirals figure prominently in Neolithic art, and I thought it reasonable to surmise that a spiral processional route up the mound was incorporated into its design.

Silbury's causeways possibly could be remnants of an earlier shallow ditch, but whatever they may be, they would have provided access to the mound across the surrounding ditches. The causeways, the proposed processional route and the flat top could reasonably be construed as indicators that Silbury was meant to be climbed. That seems inappropriate for a tomb, although it is entirely consistent with an observational or ritual platform. However, if that was the builders' intention, why did they construct a chalk 'hill' in an area of natural chalk hills of similar height (Waden and Windmill Hills are the two most similar), and with height clearly being an important criterion, why was the mound located in the deepest part of the valley?

Perspective of the landscape emerged as a possible answer. In such undulating terrain, perspective can change dramatically when an observer moves position by as little as one or two metres, with the result that hills of similar height around Silbury do not share the same view. If Silbury was designed as an observational or ritual platform, and therefore something to be looked at or from, it follows that the panorama from the summit, or its position, must have some special quality absent from natural platforms in the vicinity. Considering the mound's unprecedented height, I was surprised this hypothesis had not been fully investigated before. As stated, Paul Devereux postulated a double sunrise effect as seen from the summit and terrace on the May and August festival days, but he had examined only a small fraction of Silbury's total horizons.

If it can be assumed the mound was built for observational purposes, then a territorial role or roles are extremely likely to have been intended. There is also a possibility the mound was designed as an astronomical observatory, linking celestial events with certain features in its horizons.

There are three realistic territorial schemes to consider; intervisibility of monuments, definition of boundaries, or a combination of the two. Within those parameters the mound's location can be seen as predetermined in some way, or intrinsic to a topographical scheme. In all cases it is presumed that either extensive woodland clearances during the Mid to Late Neolithic periods or naturally occurring grassland facilitated intervisibility of sites. That is a moot point of course, although the pollen and molluscan records (Evans *et al*) indicate large tracts of grassland with very little woodland around the time of Silbury's construction, with little if any differentiation between hillsides and valley basins.

Of insect assemblages recovered from within the mound itself, all but one are open country species. At the time of writing, the very latest research at Stonehenge is indicating that southern Neolithic Britain actually had much less wooded land than previously thought.

Intervisibility of monuments.

The pre-eminent components of Avebury's later Neolithic complex are Silbury Hill, the henge, the West Kennet palisaded enclosures, the stone avenues and the avenues' termini. The site of the former stone and timber circle known as the Sanctuary is believed to mark the end (or beginning) of the West Kennet Avenue, which runs to the southern entrance of the henge. The terminus of the Beckhampton Avenue that ran from the henge's western entrance has not yet been determined, although extensive excavations carried out in 2003 produced no evidence of the avenue beyond the Longstones. The larger of two stones at this site 'Adam' is believed to have been part of an arrangement of stones known as a cove, very similar to the one in the henge's northern sector. The other stone 'Eve' is the only remaining upright stone of the avenue. There is evidence of a ditched enclosure at the site, although the cove and enclosure are probably not contemporaneous. If both avenues were designed to be of equal length at approximately one and a half miles, then the Beckhampton Avenue could not have terminated at the cove. Possibly it veered sharply from the cove towards the valley's western scarp, but William Stukeley's proposal that it continued in a south-westerly direction from the site now appears to be untenable, unless there is a considerable break in its course.

If sightlines to Silbury's contemporary monuments were deemed important, the priorities would have been the henge, the avenues, the Sanctuary and its counterpart on the Beckhampton Avenue. The palisaded enclosures excavated by Whittle at West Kennet farm are believed to be a little later than Silbury, although an overlap in the periods of usage is likely. The sites of Falkner's circle, the Winterbourne Basset stone circle and the recently discovered remains of a probable stone circle on Harestone Down also should be considered. Perhaps a visual link between old and new monuments was the aim, in which case the area's numerous long barrows and Windmill Hill's causewayed enclosures are relevant.

Beginning with the earthworks of the henge, a bank estimated to have been 7m or more in height, and a ditch up to 11m deep surrounded the henge's megalithic features. Within an outer stone circle are a southern inner circle and a northern inner circle or horseshoe. The centres of both inner features were marked by enormous megaliths; the 'Obelisk' (Stukeley) in the southern and the 'Cove' in the northern. It is reasonable to assume these two sites were foci for ritual and ceremonial activities within the henge, and therefore targets for Silbury's sightlines.

Contrary to the observation made in the English Heritage guide to Avebury, Silbury *is* visible from within the henge. The great mound can be seen from various locations in the northern sector, and if modern buildings were removed, it would be visible from the Cove in the northern inner feature. Most interestingly, from vantage points around the Obelisk in the southern inner circle, only Silbury's summit platform is visible above the western slope of Waden Hill.

Picture 3. Silbury's summit platform from the henge.

It presents quite a remarkable sight, and it certainly appears that the mound was located and built to the necessary height in order to bring the Obelisk and the Cove into view.

Little of the West Kennet Avenue is visible from the mound, although its terminus at the Sanctuary can be seen clearly. The course of the now demolished Beckhampton Avenue would have been visible as it left the henge's western entrance, but the avenue's cove at the Longstones would not. If the cove did indeed mark the avenue's terminus, it would be a conspicuous omission from Silbury's view.

The most telling evidence in the case of intervisibility of contemporaneous monuments is not found at the monuments themselves, but at the natural platform of Waden Hill. Silbury as an observational platform playing a pivotal role in the interconnection of the complex probably would not have been its builders' intention, for a clearer view of the complex is available from the northern end of Waden Hill's flat top. More of the henge interior and the West Kennet Avenue are revealed, the Sanctuary also is clearly visible, as are the Longstones and the course of the Beckhampton Avenue. The terminus of the Beckhampton Avenue would have been visible, either at the cove or elsewhere. The Winterbourne Basset stone circle and Harestone Down are visible from both Silbury and Waden Hills, but Falkner's circle can only be seen from Waden. A suitable site for observing other monuments and their ritual gatherings could have been designed on Waden Hill with relatively little effort, rendering the colossal undertaking of Silbury Hill unnecessary. Before we can have confidence in that conclusion, two more sightlines must be considered.

The sites of the former West Kennet palisaded enclosures are not visible from the northern end of Waden Hill, although they are close to Silbury and would have been clearly visible from it. Even if the enclosures did not exist at the time of Silbury's construction, they could have been planned or the location itself could have been deemed important. The enclosures formed a huge complex of monuments, mainly consisting of three structures up to 340m in width that spread over a large area of the river's flood plain. There can be no doubt they were seen as being very important, especially if the present course of the river at that particular point is the same as its Neolithic course, for the river actually would have run through one of the enclosures. Even so, it seems highly unlikely that intervisibility with them would have motivated the construction of Silbury, as the *southern* summit area and slopes of Waden Hill provide ideal locations to look down on the enclosures' sites.

Secondly, the Sanctuary stood on a prime site on the Ridgeway's high ground which could have marked the spot where any travellers from the east would first see Silbury, thus placing them on the border of the great mound's 'domain'. The West Kennet Avenue ceremonial route could have started there for that reason. If this speculative role is applied to the Beckhampton Avenue, it follows that travellers from the west would be provided with a similar ceremonial route from the point where Silbury came into their view. Numerous locations near the western scarp would have sufficed, one of which is Knoll Down on the course of the Old Bath Road. As Miller and Broadhurst pointed out, a counterpart to the Sanctuary at the right spot on Knoll Down would be precisely aligned with Silbury and the Sanctuary, and each avenue terminus would appear from their counterpart to 'sit' on Silbury's platform. There appear to be unrecorded earthworks on the relevant part of Knoll Down, although one must question whether visual alignment would be sufficient motivation for the immense effort that Silbury's construction must have entailed. Only the intervisibility of a platform with Knoll Down and the Sanctuary would have been necessary, not the precise linear arrangement of the sites.

In the case of a possible visual link between old and contemporary monuments, Waden Hill once again is a stronger candidate than Silbury. The causewayed enclosures on Windmill Hill are visible from both vantage points, but more long barrows are visible from Waden than Silbury, and Waden's horizons encompass territory that contains more.

Territorial boundaries.

Environmental records indicate there was little woodland in the Late Neolithic Silbury landscape, although we cannot know exactly which areas were clear of trees during the relevant period. Acid rain and ploughing have had some effect on ground levels over the last four to five thousand years, yet could not have reduced ground contours sufficiently to alter Silbury's horizons. Using contours as a guide, and with all buildings and modern plantations effectively removed from the landscape, the red lines on the map represent the horizons visible from Silbury's 187m OD platform, with an extra 2m allowed for the height of an observer and a slight amount of inevitable erosion. Curvature of the Earth was entered into all the calculations, and where clear sightlines still exist they were checked in the field and found to be drawn accurately on the map. Please note that not all the ground between Silbury and its visible horizons can necessarily be seen from the summit platform. Undulating terrain inevitably obscures some sections of ground, as they are hidden behind knolls and hillocks.

To the north-west (not included on the map) the Cotswold Hills are marginally visible, but they are around twenty miles beyond the steep escarpment that clearly defines the western limit of Silbury's local environs, and could not have entered any consideration of local territorial boundaries.

Remarkably, the southern horizon on the map sweeps all the way to the east beyond Marlborough. If the mound was territorial in the sense of claiming territory, its builders were laying claim to a disproportionate sector of ground south of the river compared to ground north of it. The horizons to the south-west are the most interesting of all. If Silbury had a territorial purpose, why are King's Play and Roundway Hills not in view? Both are sections of the uniquely distinct escarpment that surrounds the Winterbourne/Kennet Valley to the south, west and north. To the east, the Ridgeway completes the clearly defined, natural 'walls' of the zone. The escarpment is so pronounced it resembles the ramparts of a castle when viewed from outside of the valley. If definition of territorial boundaries was the aim, why would a section of this most obvious natural boundary be ignored? Neolithic soil levels were up to one metre higher than at present, and erosion of the underlying chalk has occurred, but by nothing like enough to make King's Play and Roundway Hills disappear from

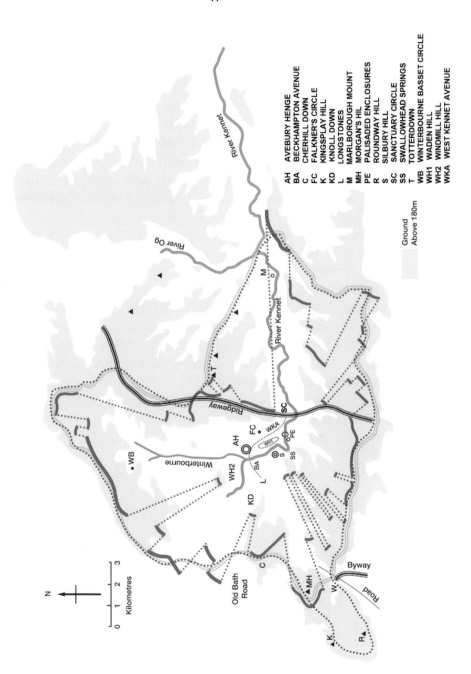

AH   AVEBURY HENGE
BA   BECKHAMPTON AVENUE
C   CHERHILL DOWN
FC   FALKNER'S CIRCLE
K   KINGSPLAY HILL
KD   KNOLL DOWN
L   LONGSTONES
M   MARLBOROUGH MOUNT
MH   MORGAN'S HIL
PE   PALISADED ENCLOSURES
R   ROUNDWAY HILL
S   SILBURY HILL
SC   SANCTUARY CIRCLE
SS   SWALLOWHEAD SPRINGS
T   TOTTERDOWN
WB   WINTERBOURNE BASSET CIRCLE
WH1 WADEN HILL
WH2 WINDMILL HILL
WKA WEST KENNET AVENUE

Ground
Above 180m

Map 1

Silbury's view. As a territorial 'claim' therefore, the panorama from Silbury is totally impractical. Evidently, the recognition of obvious natural boundaries was not in the builders' thoughts, although a more subtle form of territorial division does seem to be indicated.

The double blue line with dots on the map is the water-catchment area for the River Kennet down to its confluence with the River Og at Marlborough. The solely dotted blue line forming a spur in the south-western sector is included in the catchment area on Environment Agency maps, but it is a very problematical sector. It is also the 'missing' sightline area of King's Play and Roundway Hills.

Contours on Ordnance Survey maps indicate that rainfall on the spur would be drawn eastward to a steep decline beginning at the top of the byway, then to the south and away from the River Kennet. Although to modern observers at the site it appears the ground surface generally declines towards Silbury and the river, that impression would change dramatically if the road and its substantial verge were removed. Surface water would flow from the spur to the area marked 'W', and from there it could drain along either of the direction indicators shown in map 2.

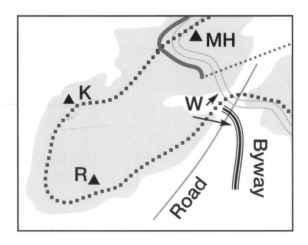

Map 2

Rainfall in the chalk uplands filters down to the water-table, allowing hardly any surface run-off. The highest ground in Wiltshire forms the valley's southern boundary, yet not a single stream issues from it. Only after prolonged and extremely heavy rainfall would any streams have appeared here, apart from streams issuing from springs. Springs are active when fluctuating subterranean water levels reach the required height, and that is dependent on topography, geology and the scale of the water-catchment area. Whatever the reason for the spur's omission from Silbury's view, modern borehole technology has proven my blue line boundary to be the true catchment area, for the Environment Agency's borehole results demonstrate that the spur's groundwater actually drains to the south and west, and therefore away from Silbury and the River Kennet.

There can be no doubt that water would have been of paramount importance to Neolithic communities living on the chalk downs, and a water supply emanating from the ground in the form of springs even in dry weather would certainly have been treated reverentially. A practical and religious motive for the mound's construction could be indicated, with springs and the catchment area that fed them being deemed sacred or at least highly providential. If the mound builders appreciated the unusual or possibly even unique interaction of the topography and hydrology of the area, it could explain why King's Play and Roundway Hills were excluded from Silbury's view, for they lie outside its water-catchment area. To the north-east of Silbury beyond the apparent natural boundary of the Ridgeway, Totterdown could have been included in Silbury's panorama because it forms part of the watershed. Continuing on that theme, the southern horizon from Silbury's platform is seen to sweep all the way around to Marlborough because it conforms to the watershed, and then continues a short distance entirely within the ongoing river valley.

All local terrain visible from Silbury Hill lies within the River Kennet's direct water-catchment area, and the horizons visible from the mound are often compatible with the watersheds. That is not the case from any natural vantage points in the area, all of which have sightlines over the valley's surrounding ridges into other local catchment areas. King's Play and Roundway Hills would have been the first non-catchment sectors to come into view as the mound rose in height, and Silbury appears to have been taken right up to their threshold. If the mound was just 2m higher, Roundway Hill would have been in view above Bishop's Canning Down, and at 3m higher King's Play Hill would have been visible above the southern slope of Morgan's Hill.

It could be argued that such sightlines would be the inevitable result of any mound located deep within the bowl of a valley, although that would presume a more or less consistent height of surrounding ground, which is definitely not the case here. Either by chance or design, Silbury's location and height utilise the undulating nature of its surroundings. If that occurred simply by chance, the great mound's platform presents the optimum position to view as much of the River Kennet's water-catchment area as possible *and no further* by a quite astonishing coincidence. I am sure that readers will understand why I was excited by that discovery, and why I considered it to be a genuine 'eureka' moment.

As for the distant sector of the Cotswold Hills that can be seen from Silbury, the archaeologist David Field has made the interesting observation that the source of the River Thames is in the Cotswolds, and that the River Kennet is a tributary of the Thames. The Cotswolds are the only ground in Silbury's panorama that does not belong to the mound's water catchment area, which again seems to be an intriguing coincidence.

There is, of course, a possibility that Silbury's location was in some way predetermined and not the result of a topographical plan. The mound stands in a slightly elevated position at the end of a very long chalk spur projecting into low-lying gravels. Such a promontory naturally would have attracted attention. Research published by Steve Marshall in 2013 emphasised this, and will be described later. Also, Silbury's position close to the source of the River Kennet at Swallowhead Springs could be an indication of its builders' intentions. The earliest written reference found to the upper limit of the river is from Leyland, one of Henry VIII's chroniclers. He noted "the Kennet riseth north-north west as Silbury

Hill bottom." Therefore, it is possible the mound marked an earlier source of the river. In either case, it seems unlikely that Silbury's summit platform would be at an elevation and location where the water-catchment area is seen to optimum effect simply by chance.

One further possible reason for a predetermined or providential location relates to the monument's ditch. It was not until 2001 that the archaeological establishment began to concede that Silbury's ditch could have been designed to flood. Before that date, conventional 'wisdom' had it that the ditch was dry, even though that would have required a Late Neolithic water-table much lower than at present.

Evidence that had been interpreted as supporting the 'dry ditch' hypothesis can be found in an extensive ecological study (Evans *et al*), and in Professor Richard Atkinson's findings from his ditch cuttings in the 1968 excavations. The Evans report concludes that the river valley upstream of the Swallowhead Springs (the Winterbourne) was completely dry at the time of Silbury's construction until alluvium was deposited in seasonal floodwater, thereby creating rivers in the immediate vicinity *c.*2300 to 2250 BC (the West Overton Formation). It should be noted that the report's authors found those events difficult to explain, although they are consistent with the climate history, which indicates slightly warmer and drier conditions at the time of Silbury's construction than at present. Conversely, the Evans report also states that in the Late Neolithic the water-table was rising.

From the mound itself, excavated fauna include two waterfowl, two beaver and some frog fragments. Aquatic habitats are evident in the mosses recovered from the primary mound, and large amounts of freshwater snails were found in the ditch cutting that flooded before Atkinson's excavation reached the bottom of the ditch. As the original ditch could not have been dug underwater, it was concluded the Late Neolithic water-table was lower than at present, and that Silbury's ditch must have been dry. However, Atkinson should have expected the cutting to flood. In 1886, Alfred Pass noted that even after a long dry summer, water stood to a depth of 2.5m in his ditch shafts. Atkinson also excavated the ditch in the summer when the water-table is still sinking after winter saturation.

Figures taken from the closest Water Board borehole to Silbury from which data is available (approximately 1.5 km north-west of the mound), clearly indicate that a November cutting by Atkinson would have remained dry, and that any ditch over 2m deep in the vicinity would be prone to flooding when the aquifer is higher in the summer months.

Misinterpretation of the nature of the water-table has formed the basis of a fundamentally flawed argument, and caused some confusion among the authorities. Environmental evidence from the Evans report indicates only that Silbury's immediate surroundings were dry on the surface before construction of the mound, and even that is contradicted by a more recent English Heritage internet report. It describes results from a geophysical and seismic survey, which "not only serves to emphasize the enormous size of the mound, but also its lowland setting on the very edge of dry chalkland immediately adjacent to water. Whether this water flowed freely or intermittently during the period of the monument's construction and use is not known." Alasdair Whittle has discussed the environment of the mound and the downstream palisaded enclosures. "At least it is not certain that the enclosures were traversed by an active watercourse, nor that the ditch around Silbury Hill would have been filled regularly from such a watercourse." (*Sacred Mound, Holy Rings*, Oxbow 1997.)

In fact, neither a watercourse nor any other surface water would have been necessary for Silbury's ditch to flood, because the subterranean aquifer did so. The ditch is believed to have been up to 10m deep before it filled with silt. Under present conditions with an annual water-table fluctuation of about 8m, if the silt in the ditch was removed, it would flood to a depth of at least 5m or possibly 6m in February or March, and remain wet for at least eight months.

The water-table generally is most accessible in the deepest part of any valley. Silbury's ditch is in the basin of a very large chalk valley where the highest level of groundwater accumulates. There is no evidence the nearby Swallowhead Springs were active in the Late Neolithic, but the top of Silbury's ditch is at the same contour level as the springs, which are activated by subterranean groundwater. In the south-west ditch terminal, a well or spring was still in use as late as the 19th century. In addition, the slightly drier Late Neolithic climate would not necessarily have had a marked effect on the water-table level.

Silbury was built during the Sub Boreal phase of Britain's climate history when temperatures were approximately those of today, and it was slightly drier. "However, those descriptions are relative to the preceding Atlantic phase. In the Atlantic period it was both wetter and warmer than at present. Thus conditions when Silbury was built may not have differed much from today, but they had been preceded by a long period of wet conditions. The chalk downs form an aquifer of great capacity, theoretically therefore, springs in the third millennium BC would be more numerous and higher up the valleys than today." (Chris Joseph, former head of geography at Marlborough College, pers comm.)

Water-table levels during the Sub Boreal phase would have fallen from those of the wetter Atlantic phase, although rainfall and thus water-table levels were rising again at the time of Silbury's construction. For the ditch to have remained dry throughout the year in the period of the monument's usage, the water-table would have required an annual range no less than 5m lower than at present, and all that in an age before the extensive modern practise of water extraction from the aquifer by pumping. The preceding Atlantic period should have counterbalanced the effect on water-table levels of the slightly drier Late Neolithic climate, rendering a 5m difference unlikely. A water-table at that level, and the climate in the interim from the mound's construction to the proposed date of the West Overton Formation, would not be conducive to flooding and creation of the Winterbourne in the relatively brief period indicated by the Evans report. For the West Overton Formation to have occurred, the water-table must have been high. With a high water-table, Silbury's ditch could not possibly have been dry.

Environmental evidence of a dry valley does not preclude the existence of a flooded ditch. If water is the key to understanding the monument, its location could have been determined by a desire for its ditch to flood, thus echoing the proposed theme of its panorama. That could offer an explanation for the long and shallow western extension of the ditch. The Neolithic workers may have been intent on completing the mound at a time of year when the water-table was rising and was too high to facilitate deeper quarrying. That would be consistent with completion of the project in the winter when farming communities could devote their time to construction, rather than to agriculture and animal husbandry.

As previously stated, an estimated three million man-hours would have been required to quarry the 239,000 cubic metres of material and construct the mound. Very recently, it has been discovered that up to 4,000 people may have been gathering annually at Durrington Walls to celebrate the Winter Solstice at Stonehenge. Masses of animal bones left over from feasting have been analysed and found to prove that animals were brought to Durrington Walls from as far afield as Orkney! The festivities took place at the same time that Stonehenge's sarsen circle and horseshoe were constructed, so it appears that major building projects may have been supported to some extent by the entire British population. If that also happened at Silbury Hill, a workforce of 1,000 people spending two winter months at the site could have completed the work in just six years. Alternatively, the same number of people could have built the mound in just one year if they stayed on site for the whole twelve months. Archaeologists prefer to think of Silbury as a project that was spread over a number of generations, but no matter how unlikely it may seem, a time period for construction from one to six years is within the parameters of the radiocarbon dates described in part 6.

In 2001, a feature that resembles a drainage ditch became evident as a vegetation mark when the ditch extension dried out completely at the base. It appeared to lead from the south-western corner where the old spring or well used to be, and could have been intended to channel its water into the main ditch. Because of this feature and other factors, David Field has concluded, "It seems likely then, that Silbury Hill's ditches were intentionally filled with water." (*Great Sites*, British Archaeology, May 2003.) An English Heritage internet report refers to the same feature and states "the importance of the drainage system to the construction and symbolic meaning of Silbury is undeniable."

The 'wet or dry' debate was finally put to bed in 2013 by the brilliant research of Steve Marshall (*British Archaeology*, July/August, 2013 issue 131). A little earlier in 2012, Paul Whitehead and Mike Edmunds of the School of Geography and the Environment at Oxford University had conducted research supported by English Heritage into Silbury's palaeohydrology – how groundwater, springs and rivers might have appeared when the mound was built. They concluded the water-table at the time could have been 5m higher than at present. Later research by other archaeologists brings the 5m figure into doubt, and now most of them favour a figure of 2m. Inevitably, that would have caused flooding of Silbury's ditch in the Late Neolithic, and Steve Marshall's findings were to prove even more illuminating.

For five years, culminating in 2012 when torrential rain caused the River Kennet to burst its banks, he amassed evidence of a vast network of springs in the Silbury area that had previously been unknown. Ultimately, he discovered no fewer than 89 springs in Silbury's ditch itself, and that the present course of the Kennet is not its original one. Temperature readings of the spring waters showed they are at 10°C all year round, considerably warmer than surface water caused by precipitation, and warm enough to melt the snow and ice that formed around the ditch in the winter of 2012. Incredibly, that resulted in a green belt of still-growing grass around the monument, leading Steve Marshall to write, "It is not hard to imagine why Silbury's location may have been regarded as special. With its springs and two steaming spring-fed rivers, it must have been a magical place – one of verdant fertility and perpetual springtime, even in the depths of winter." (ibid.)

Without putting too fine a point on this, neither is it hard to imagine why the Kennet's original name should have been in use as late as the 18th century, as 'Cunnit' is an entirely appropriate name for a river that arose from a warm, wet and fertile place. According to Michael Dames and Julian Cope, the name is derived from the once reverential and now profane word you are thinking of, as is the name of the nearby Roman settlement of Cunetio.

In conclusion regarding the various aspects of Silbury's panorama, if the mound was intended to fulfil observational or ritual roles, it probably was not constructed solely as a platform to view contemporary monuments or their ceremonial and ritual gatherings. Neither is it likely to have served as a prominent ceremonial platform itself, nor as a visual link between old and contemporary monuments, as the natural platform of Waden Hill could have fulfilled all those roles more effectively.

As a platform designed to view and thus 'claim' territory, Silbury would have been impractical, but the horizons visible from its platform hint at a quasi-religious motive for its construction, based on the valley's water-catchment area and springs. The mound could have been a monument to its builders' appreciation and reverence for the unusual topography and hydrology of the region, and the bounty that it yielded. That bounty would have been manifest in the fertility of the land, the highly providential springs and that most precious Neolithic commodity of flint, in which the Kennet's water-catchment area is quite astonishingly rich. Under such circumstances it would have been appropriate for the mound's ditch to be designed to flood, which is now a certainty regardless of whatever the mound's purpose actually may have been.

The very least that can be said is that the mound's platform is at the optimum height and location for the proposed territorial role. That assumes, of course, that Silbury's present height is very close to its original and intended one.

The Astronomy.

If the mound is at its original height, could the platform have been designed for astronomical observations? Few stellar alignments have been claimed to exist at Neolithic monuments, and as far as I am aware, none have been proven. Solar and lunar alignments would almost certainly have been considered to be of greater importance.

Since 2500 BC, both the sun and moon's limiting declinations have changed by about 0.5°, which is roughly equal to the width of their discs. The alignments in the appendix are all for the period around 2500 BC, which is close enough to Silbury's date of construction for astronomical calculations. All solar calculations are based on the first flash of the rising sun and the final sighting of its disappearing disc. As anyone who has ever watched a sunrise knows (which is surprisingly few of us), the first flash of the sun's upper limb is unmistakable and similar to seeing a car's headlights appear over the brow of a hill. Because of the brightness of the sun, it is impossible for the naked eye to judge accurately when its exact centre is on the horizon or when its full disc first appears to sit on the skyline. With the moon the sightings are easier, although the positions of its first and last glimpses would still have been the most recognisable, and therefore most likely to have been chosen by Neolithic observers.

As the appendix clearly demonstrates, Silbury Hill was not constructed with solar or lunar alignments in mind.

Silbury Hill and Marlborough Mount.

There is a conspicuous gap in the Silbury watershed sightlines. To the east of the mound and north of the River Kennet, the Manton Down/Barton Down ridge is hidden behind the Ridgeway. In order to bring the missing ridge into view, the ideal observation platform should have been located south or south-east of Silbury's position, but no suitable location or elevation exists that could match the catchment area visible from Silbury without also seeing non-catchment ground beyond it. It appears the mound builders had no choice other than to leave the ridge out of sight, and that Silbury was the sole instrument of the proposed territorial scheme. However, there is a strong probability that Silbury had a partner or acolyte mound.

A little over five miles downriver from Silbury in the grounds of Marlborough College, there is another large mound known as the Marlborough Mount that is ideally placed to 'pick up the baton' from Silbury's sightlines. The Mount is designated on maps as a motte, and although it was certainly incorporated into a Norman motte and bailey castle, that does not preclude an earlier provenance. Although smaller than Silbury, there are striking similarities between the two mounds. Both are conical in shape and situated close to river confluences at the foot of chalk spurs. Deep ditches originally surrounded both mounds, and it is known that a spring-fed stream flooded Marlborough Mount's ditch, which has subsequently been infilled. Its position beneath the steep slopes of Marlborough Common is unusual among motte sites, which were chosen for their prominent locations.

A report by Joanne Best stated the Mount is probably medieval but could be Neolithic. A more recent investigation by David Field *et al* came out heavily in favour of a medieval date, although conceding that the Norman construction could cover a prehistoric mound. That would be consistent with findings at other mottes, which are enlarged mounds of prehistoric or Roman date.

I have always believed the Mount to be Neolithic. Quite apart from its obvious geographic and physical similarities with Silbury, as Aubrey Burl wrote, "it is clearly pre-Norman. The Saxon name of Marlborough, Maerle-beorg, Maerla's mound or, arguably, 'gentian hill', must refer to it. There are no other hills nearby." (*Prehistoric Avebury*, Yale University Press 2002.) Julian Cope also believes that Marlborough is a Saxon place-name, literally translating as 'chalk mound'. How could a Norman construction have a Saxon name when the Saxons overran much of present-day England hundreds of years before the Norman invasion?

In 1912 when building work was taking place next to the mound, a portion of the western base was removed, revealing the old ground surface. Above the old turf line was a thin layer of compressed clay covered by chalk rubble, which repeats the sequence at Silbury's base perimeter. Several pieces of deer antler were recovered, some with signs of rough usage on them, which is consistent with finds at Neolithic monuments where antlers were invariably used as digging tools and then placed or discarded into the monuments. Unfortunately, the antler pieces have somehow been lost, and have never been available for radiocarbon dating.

Why was the mound used as a motte? Almost certainly because it was so conspicuous in its immediate surroundings; the Normans simply could not resist the temptation. A castle built on Marlborough Mount would have been a striking symbol of power within the settlement, and it came complete with a spring-fed moat.

The Joanne Best report states that the course of the Roman road through Marlborough cannot be traced, although it may have been roughly on the course of the present road to the north of the Mount. Information provided by Dr. Rogers, the archivist at Marlborough College, supports the northern bearing. He believes that one of Marlborough's Saxon roads came down from a north-easterly direction to meet the Roman road at a point west of the Mount on the present-day road. He points to some unusual property boundaries at the location that strongly indicate a meeting of two old roads.

To the east, heading toward the Mount but off the present road, is a site where old road foundations were discovered during building work in 1975. Further to the east beyond the Mount is the old footbridge across the River Kennet, and then the course of the Roman road on its way to the Roman town Cunetio. The line from the Roman road and the footbridge leads to a point just to the north-east of the Mount, where it is met by the line from the Saxon/Roman junction and the road foundations site. Dr. Rogers points out that those lines clearly divert around the Mount, which strongly indicates a prehistoric date. On the other hand, the existence of a handful of mottes that are similar in size to Marlborough Mount is the only evidence for a medieval date.

In 2008, an investigation was instigated by the Marlborough Mount Trust. Boreholes were driven from the top of the Mount down to the old ground surface, and samples were taken for radiocarbon analyses. It was time to place all bets, and the initial results indicated a date of 2840 BC.

For a monument that gave the town its name, the present overgrown state of the site is pitiful. The ditch has been completely filled and covered in tarmac, and its spring piped down to the river. On the top, there is a 2m deep circular pit that a 17th century landowner dug for a swimming pool and summerhouse. Currently the pit holds a large water tank, and a 20th century chimney stands above it. The Joanne Best report states that a section of the Norman castle wall is visible just below the summit, but to my untutored eye it is undetectable. The 17th century landowner cut a spiral walkway around the mound, which led up to his swimming pool. You would be hard-pushed to find any text that is complimentary of his work, although in view of the Silbury findings it is possible his walkway was actually a re-cutting of an original feature. It is believed that after the Norman castle another tower was erected on the summit, of which nothing remains.

All that interference and damage has undoubtedly shortened the Mount's height, and there are no records that offer even a clue to its original stature; quite a problem for someone wishing to plot the original sightlines. The Mount's covering of trees didn't help either. All I could do was plot sightlines at its present height by use of a map.

A 130-metre contour runs through Marlborough Mount's western base. Add the present height of 19.8m plus 1.5m for the height of an observer, and the total is 151.32m OD. I rounded that off to the nearest whole metre to ease the calculations; after all, I knew the findings could never be entirely satisfactory. Once more, curvature of the Earth was included.

From the present height of the summit platform, if the Mount was cleared of trees, the river valley and sections of the river itself would be in view to the west, in between Silbury and the Mount. Also, the 'missing' Manton down/Barton Down watershed would be clearly visible, coming into view for the first time at Totterdown, exactly at the point where it disappears from Silbury's view. Far to the west, Morgan's Hill and a section of Cherhill Down would be in view, just as they are from Silbury, so the two mounds cannot represent two separate territorial claims. That is emphasised at Silbury's most easterly horizons, which are shared with Marlborough Mount's in two sections. All that would indeed seem to indicate a relationship between the mounds.

Other than that, little can be stated with any confidence about the original sightlines from the Mount, although I can dispel one particular myth that often appears on internet postings. Silbury Hill and Marlborough Mount are not and never could have been intervisible, and therefore their east to west orientation certainly was not aligned on the equinoctial sunrises and sunsets. An extra 25m in the combined height of the mounds would be required to bring them into view of each other above the intervening ground of the Ridgeway, and that is impossible. Even if they were both perfectly conical in shape with no flattening at the pinnacles, they could never have attained such a height. And yet, at the time I was researching the mounds' sightlines, it seemed obvious to me there must be much more to the mounds' relationship than the sightlines were indicating. It could not simply be a coincidence that Britain's only two prehistoric mounds of such enormous stature were built just five miles from each other in the same river valley, but not a single researcher had ever offered a reasonable explanation. Much later, while I was carrying out an entirely new approach to my research, I realised what the relationship between the mounds actually might have been.

Part 6. The final intervention.

In the year 2000, English Heritage had their hands full trying to establish whether the hole at the top of Silbury represented the only section of the mound that required repair. Initially, they believed the great mound was generally stable and that they only needed to refill the hole, but with what? Chalk similar to the original mound deposits could confuse any future archaeological investigation, and any other material would surely be a contaminant. While they were pondering this, the situation worsened.

After a seismic survey carried out early in 2001, a number of anomalies or voids were discovered within the mound, and it was decided that a full geophysical survey was required. However, time was passing, Silbury was in danger and no visible activity was taking place. The public were getting restless, and Michael Ancram (M.P. for Devizes) urged English Heritage to act swiftly. Behind the scenes they were actually doing as much as they could, but groups such as the Ancient Sacred Landscapes Network and certain druid orders were not convinced of that, and were openly venting their frustration.

An ultra-modern method of seismic recording was available from the American company Skanska, and they were contracted to investigate and subsequently repair the mound. The initial stage of their work required a drilling rig to be erected on the top of Silbury, so English Heritage first had to arrange a temporary filling of the collapsed shaft in order to support Skanska's rig. That was achieved by lining the crater with a geotextile membrane filled with polystyrene blocks, which were then weighted down with 50 tonnes of chalk. Skanska's process involved drilling holes through the mound, filling them with water, and then setting off airgun charges. Equipment set up on the slopes of Silbury could then record responses to the charges from various depths and sections, thus generating a 3D model of the interior of the mound. The results proved there were indeed a number of voids that required attention, and it was decided there was no option but to re-enter the Atkinson tunnel to conduct a thorough process of investigation and repair. In 2006, the English Heritage Advisory Committee gave authorisation, and on 11 May 2007 – fully seven years after the summit collapse – the 1968 tunnel was re-opened. Repairs took another year to complete.

All the detected voids and the tunnel were infilled with chalk sourced from the same geological strata as the original mound. Working back from the centre to the entrance, mining arches were removed as chalk mixed with water was pumped back in, although a few arches were left in place because it was unsafe to remove them. The temporary filling on the summit was removed and similarly infilled with chalk, after the crater had been carefully archaeologically monitored.

Observations made during the 2007/8 work confirmed that topsoil on the original ground surface had been stripped before the mound was constructed, which raises a pertinent question: is that evidence of preparation of the ground for the entire mound, or simply the result of pre-mound activity? The golden, sticky gravel forming a 1m high mound at the very core of Silbury was again observed, together with its covering of a 16m diameter, waist-high mound of topsoil, subsoil and turves. The clay content of these soils and turves indicate they are the same topsoil that had been stripped before work began, and then stored nearby. That suggests the work was done quickly and to a plan. A new discovery of the outlines of two smaller mounds were seen in the tunnel walls a few metres away from the primary mound. They were both less than half a metre high and made of dark organic mud. One had a tiny gully dug around it, to quote Leary and Field: "like a small-scale model of the final Silbury." *The Story of Silbury Hill* (English Heritage 2010.)

One of the mini-mounds contained remains associated with woodland or scrub, clearly indicating that its soil had been collected from a different place than the other mini-mound and the primary mound. The soils of those contain seeds, plant remains and insects that came from mature, well-grazed grassland.

Two pits of around one metre in depth and diameter were found in the primary mound. These had been dug out and then filled with the same material pushed back in, which seems a pointless exercise, but one pit contained worked flints and the other an ants nest. They could represent a deliberate addition to the cultural and environmental archive within Silbury. As Professor Richard Atkinson had discovered in 1968, the primary mound was seen to be covered under clearly defined layers of topsoil, chalk, clay, gravel and turf. The topsoil contrasted with the clayey topsoil of the primary mound, for it had been gathered from a surface that directly overlay chalk, and therefore came from a different area. These distinctive layers formed a mound 35m in diameter, estimated to be 5m or 6m high. A large number of naturally rounded sarsen boulders were also present in this layered mound, and they had been carefully and evenly distributed throughout it: "deliberately incorporated within the body of the mound as an element of its composition...The material for these early mounds had been carefully chosen; this was no random spoil heap, but pieces of other places carefully piled high" (Leary and Field, ibid).

The Silbury builders could not have left a better archive of their environment if they had tried. It could be argued that is exactly what they intended, and it is very reminiscent of the archives left by their ancestors in the long barrows. Furthermore, this does not represent a haphazard, disjointed development of the site; it is clearly the result of a plan.

Moving out from the centre of the mound, a series of five chalk banks were seen in the tunnel walls, some mixed with clay. Previously only two of these had been reported. Although they could only be seen in profile, it is believed they are sections of rings around the central core, progressively expanding the monument outwards by a few metres at a time. If that is the case, they could have marked the perimeter of successively larger chalk mounds as Silbury II grew in height. The inner rings could have had a practical purpose in that situation, as they would have helped to stop the perimeter of each successive chalk mound from spreading as the workmen built up the conical shape of each stage of Silbury II. Without any such barriers, it would have been very difficult to achieve the angle of slope, and therefore the height required for each chalk mound. Alternatively, the rings may represent a monument in their own right, although they do not resemble any other Neolithic monument ever found. The fact they overlie the stripped ground surface also indicates they were part of the greater monument.

The outermost bank stands on the inner lip of the ditch discovered by Atkinson under Silbury III. Re-excavated in the 2007/8 investigation, the ditch was found to be 6.5m wide and 6m deep. Material from this ditch is believed to have provided the chalk and clay of the five rings and the chalk of Silbury II. Once again, although only the section of it within the tunnel can be seen, it can be surmised to be part of an enclosure around Silbury II, in which case it would have been over 100m in diameter. It was not a continuous ditch, as its base was seen to rise steeply to the west, probably marking an entranceway into an enclosure. That would be consistent with the segmented sections of ditches around Neolithic causewayed enclosures.

As Atkinson had remarked, the unweathered sides of the ditch demonstrate it had never been left open for long before being backfilled. In fact, it had been backfilled and re-cut slightly further out. This process had been repeated at least three times, moving successively outwards. Perhaps this was in order to accommodate the rapidly expanding chalk mound within it, but that would indicate a woeful lack of foresight or planning: "Whatever the reason, the process of backfilling the ditches would have required as much material put back in them as would have ever been removed in the first place, implying that they were not just simple quarries for material, but something altogether less functional. Early Neolithic causewayed enclosures frequently display such episodic backfilling and re-cutting." (Leary and Field, ibid.) "Less functional" must surely mean symbolic. Nevertheless, Leary and Field believe the constant adjustments to Silbury and its contents are evidence there was no fixed plan. I find that surprising; for me the evidence indicates quite the contrary.

The stripped surface of the original ground level beneath Silbury is evident along the full length of the tunnel and in Petrie's eastern excavation. If it was stripped all at once, and the amount of turves and soil within the primary mound suggests that it was, then the builders must have prepared the ground for the mound we see today. More importantly, the entirely impractical process of backfilling and re-cutting the ditches that now lie beneath the monument indicate the builders were creating not only an archive of Silbury's environment, but that the mound was also the embodiment of their belief systems. The symbolic causewayed enclosure beneath Silbury would thus sanctify and empower the monument in much the same way as cruciform architecture sanctifies the cathedrals and churches of more modern times.

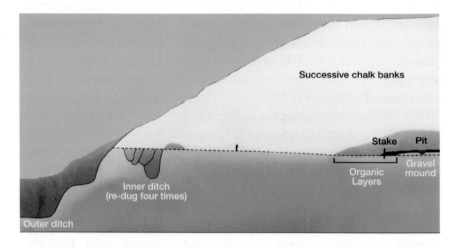

Figure 4. After English Heritage's information board at Silbury Hill, showing the position of the re-cut ditches with a human figure to scale.

Much as I like the sound of that, I must confess there may be an entirely more prosaic explanation for the covered ditches: they could simply have been for drainage, and possibly have been linked to the outer ditch by further ditches in the promontory base. The reason we cannot see any such ditches is that they would now be overgrown. I remember that my old school groundsman drained our playing fields in the same way. Fortunately for the more romantically inclined of us, that does not explain why the inner ditches were re-dug three times, as the first ditch would have sufficed. Also, such a drainage system would imply that the builders had some experience of building enormous mounds and then subsequently seeing them erode, but as far as anyone knows, there was never anything like Silbury prior to its construction.

The 2007/8 investigation also discovered that Silbury is not actually rounded. It was built in a series of straight lengths, with each length probably constructed within radial spines and buttresses formed by chalk walls (the spider's web once more). There are possibly as many as nine lengths at the base, although that figure may change further up the mound. On the summit platform, a trench was excavated which revealed the series of revetment walls in concentric rings that Atkinson had previously uncovered. These held in place layers of horizontally dumped crushed chalk. Most interestingly, there appeared to be no definite finish to these prehistoric features, and there were no later layers covering them "only the Neolithic mound and a disturbed soil horizon – nothing else." (Leary and Field, ibid.) That brings into question whether the summit is at its original height, as the damaged revetment walls indicate it would have been higher. Leary and Field have suggested it may not have been flat, but rounded. With hindsight, and in the light of the landscape discoveries to be described in the following pages, I now believe that Leary and Field are correct, and the top of Silbury was indeed rounded. If that truly was the case, then the builders may not have intended the watershed sightlines I described as being visible from the flattened summit. If the added height of the rounded summit exceeded two metres, the correct perspective would have been lost. Unfortunately, we just do not know the facts of the matter and probably never will.

The remedial work of 2007/8 provided an ideal opportunity to gather multiple samples for radiocarbon dating. The results were published (at long last) in Silbury Hill. The largest prehistoric mound in Europe (Edited by Leary, Field and Campbell, English heritage 2013). Purely scientific dating information from the radiocarbon results was analysed in accordance with the 'Bayesian' approach for interpreting chronology of the site. That is, the stratigraphic relationship between samples and the context in which they were found. Inevitably, this produced "interpretative estimates, which can and will change as further data become available and as other researchers choose to model the existing data from different perspectives." (Ibid.)

Nevertheless, the new radiocarbon results are remarkably consistent. 5 measurements dated in 2007 do not vary by more than 11 years. 21 measurements dated in 2009/10 are all within a 190 years period. 4 different models for the chronology of Silbury were produced, with the "preferred" model placing completion of the primary mound in the late 25th or early 24th centuries BC. The same model indicates that it took anywhere between 1 and 160 years to build Silbury, and most significantly, "this means that once building of Silbury started it continued at a fairly uniform rate until it was finished." (Ibid.) A table of estimates for the dates of construction events at the site shows a calibrated date range of 2460-2375 BC for both the primary mound and the final mound. The date of 2840 BC that was first announced for the Marlborough Mount also has been amended, and a date of 2400 BC for both mounds is now considered likely.

Enlightening as that may be, it does not really matter, and neither does the true height of Silbury's original summit. It is much more important to ask whether or not the Neolithic people always had an idea of how the mound eventually would appear once they had started to build it. The answer must be that they did, for if Silbury is not a tomb or an observation platform, the complexity of its construction indicates there can be only one other option. First and foremost, Silbury Hill is an effigy…

On the road that I have taken,
One day, walking, I awaken

Dean Koontz

Part 7. Revelation.

It was an unseasonably bright and warm November day in 2010, a Saturday I think. There had been few sunny weekend days that year, and I was determined not to waste it. High ground was calling, but where exactly should I go, the Marlborough Downs? How about the Cotswolds? By some process that I do not fully understand, the car found its own way to Avebury as it often does, and then continued through East Kennet village up to the pass between Milk and Knap Hills that overlooks the beautiful Vale of Pewsey. The Tan Hill Way leads eastwards from there along a high ridge that offers some of the finest views in Wiltshire, and I had just started to climb Knap Hill when I saw something in the landscape that stopped me in my tracks. No more than a mile and a half away, down in the vale, I could have sworn that I could see Silbury and Waden Hills, and that Waden had sprouted a brand new clump of trees on its summit. It appeared that the great mound and its accompanying hill had somehow been transported to another valley.

I knew that Silbury and Waden were actually situated in the Kennet Valley to the north, not to the south where I was looking. A quick glance at the map told me that 'Silbury' was in fact Pecked Hill, and 'Waden' was Woodborough Hill. I was totally bemused about never having noticed them before, as I had been to Knap Hill many times. They are even featured in Julian Cope's book, and somehow I had missed the reference or forgotten it. It was the very dark cloud shadow passing over them that made them stand out so clearly in the otherwise brightly lit valley. In fact, they appeared quite black and unnaturally monumental. Intrigued as I was, I decided there was nothing else for it but to turnabout and climb north-west up to the highest ground in the county on Milk Hill's ridge. I thought I should be able to find somewhere on the ridge where I could look north to Silbury and Waden Hills, then south to Pecked and Woodborough Hills, to check how similar they appeared. I found the right spot alongside the Wansdyke Path approximately 1km west of Red Shore where the Wansdyke crosses the Ridgeway. Once again I was in for a surprise; Silbury was as obvious as ever, but I could not see Waden Hill.

My map showed that I should be looking down along the long axis of Waden Hill and that it should be unmistakable, standing slightly to the east of Silbury. A clearly delineated hill that rises 41m above its immediate surroundings had ostensibly vanished. It was an illusion, of course, caused by the blending of the hill's outline with surrounding modern field systems. The result was by far the most effective 'camouflage' I had ever seen, and it was only when another cloud shadow passed over it that Waden's silhouette became visible. Another observation quickly became obvious; Silbury and Waden Hills did not merely appear similar to Pecked and Woodborough Hills, from my vantage point they were practically identical. Picture 4 is Silbury and Waden from the Wandsdyke, picture 5 is a closer view of Pecked and Woodborough from Knap Hill showing an identical perspective to that seen from the Wandsdyke.

Picture 4. Cloud shadow on Silbury and Waden Hills.

Picture 5. Pecked and Woodborough Hills.

The ability to recognize landmarks from different perspectives and distances must have been an essential skill for the Neolithic people. They did not have GPS systems or anything that we would recognise as portable, detailed maps. Their capacity to 'mind-map' must have been highly developed, just as it is today among many aboriginal peoples. The Late Neolithic population of Britain were used to travelling long distances, both at sea and inland. That is evident in the Cumbrian stone axes that were traded throughout Britain and Northern Europe. The Stonehenge Riverside Project has found evidence that livestock brought from as far as the Orkneys were feasted upon at Durrington Walls henge, so navigating their way through the landscape obviously did not present any problem to Neolithic travellers, and the most noticeable features in any landscape are the hills.

It is absolutely inconceivable that the people who built Silbury Hill alongside Waden Hill were unaware they had replicated a natural hill configuration located in the very next valley, especially as both configurations appear to be twins from the Milk Hill ridge. Being the highest ground in the region, the views from Milk Hill would have been very well known. Even more intriguingly, the most advantageous locations to view the configurations are the other Neolithic monuments, particularly the causewayed enclosures on Knap Hill and Windmill Hill, the Sanctuary stone circle and Harestone Down. From Knap Hill, the Pecked and Woodborough Hills feature lies south, while from Windmill Hill the Silbury and Waden Hills feature is south-east. The archaeological record clearly shows that causewayed enclosures were constructed for ritual gatherings "to act as a seasonal assembly-place for scattered communities coming from miles away for feasting, sub-tribal pacts, slaughtering of over-numerous livestock..." (Aubrey Burl, *Prehistoric Avebury,* Yale University Press 2002), and these two neighbouring enclosures overlook hill configurations of extraordinarily similar appearance.

The Windmill Hill enclosures were constructed many centuries before Silbury Hill. Artefacts and bones recovered from the enclosure ditches indicate usage of the monument from around 3700 BC with primary usage ending about two hundred years later. The most comprehensive report on Windmill Hill is Alasdair Whittle's *The Harmony of Symbols* (Oxbow 1999), which states that the enclosures witnessed repeated activity from the fourth to the early second millennia BC. "This in itself is something rather exceptional in the local record... It is evidence that people were repeatedly drawn back to the hill, probably because of the associations the enclosure continued to hold." (Ibid.) In *Windmill Hill and Avebury* (Oxford Clarendon Press 1965), Isobel Smith wrote, "It is evident that the site still continued to attract visitors even after the ditches were more or less completely filled in." Most interestingly, referring to a time between 2820 and 2660 BC, Jim Leary and David Field wrote in *The Story of Silbury Hill* "the already ancient Windmill Hill causewayed enclosure witnessed re-use." That fits the time-frame originally postulated by Professor Richard Atkinson for the construction of Silbury. Also, the fact that people still gathered at Windmill Hill long after Silbury had been built is evident in the Early Bronze Age round barrows on its summit and southern slope.

Anyone who doubts that the hill figures were deemed integral to the Windmill Hill and Knap Hill enclosures' panoramas should visit the sites; I guarantee it will give them pause for thought. No photograph can recreate the sense of recognition or *déjà vu* generated by a personal viewing.

Directly overlooking the Vale of Pewsey, Knap Hill's causewayed enclosure undoubtedly would have been used by people from the vale, and they would have invited their neighbours from the Kennet Valley to their festivities. The invitation would have been reciprocated, and once Silbury had been built, the identical hill configuration visible from both enclosures would have seemed like a home from home to the travellers. It should also be remembered there would always have been a Silbury figure, albeit of much lesser stature, formed by the mound's natural promontory base. Construction of the mound simply enhanced what was already there.

Picture 6. Silbury and Waden Hills from the Windmill Hill enclosures.

As stated, the builders of the great Silbury mound must have known that by placing it adjacent to Waden Hill they were replicating the hill figure presented by Pecked and Woodborough Hills. Therefore, the builders must have *deliberately* replicated it. The question is why? What could have been so significant about that shape? I knew the answer on the November day when I first became aware of it, for in 2006 I had travelled to the Callanish stone circle in the Western Isles to see the Southern Major rising of the moon. At Callanish, that lunar event rises from the heart of one of the most extraordinary landscape features in Britain.

Located on the remote Islands of Lewis and Harris that actually constitute one island (something to do with local rivalry I believe), Callanish stands firmly within Lewis in a stunning setting between sea-lochs. It is one of the finest stone circles in Britain. Arguably, it is also the best preserved, as it was not until 1857 that Sir James Matheson cleared the site of multiple layers of peat. For up to five millennia the peat had grown to obscure all but the tops of the stones, with the up-side being that the peat had provided protection for the prehistoric structure, and what a structure! The ground plan of the circle and its short avenues resembles a Celtic cross, although they pre-date the Christian era by almost three millennia. The stones are crystalline Lewissean gneiss, up to 5m tall, and generally very slender. Its aesthetic appeal notwithstanding, the most captivating quality of Callanish lies in its traditions and their relationship with the land and sky.

Incredible as this may seem, in 21 BC, the Roman scholar Diodurus Siculus quoted from an even earlier and now lost history by Hecatus of Abdera, which describes a voyage made by a Greek navigator and explorer known as Pytheas. The voyage is reported to have been undertaken at sometime between 330 and 238 BC. Siculus wrote that Pytheas had sailed around northern Britain, and had seen a "magnificent sacred precinct" and "notable temple" on an island "no smaller than Sicily." Pytheas had observed "the moon as viewed from this island appears to be but a little distance from the earth." The moon "god" visited the island "every nineteen years", and the island was inhabited by "Hyperboreans."

The Siculus text was first rediscovered in the early 18th century by John Toland, who placed emphasis on the text's references to harps, the transit of the moon, the spherical temple and the peculiar dialect of the Hyperboreans. To Toland, all of those were clear descriptions of the Lewis islanders and the Callanish stone circle. He also pointed out that the reference to Sicily would equate with "the great island of Lewis and Harris, with its appendages, and the adjacent Island of Skye." The "god" that visits every 19 years is the decisive factor; that is undoubtedly a reference to the 18.61-year cycle of the moon, which at the Lewis latitude of 58° north is seen to skim the horizon when it rises and falls at its southern extremes.

According to Aubrey Burl, the latitude is critical; there is no other spherical temple or sacred precinct in northern Europe that could fit the bill. At any site further north, the moon would not be seen to rise at all, and any further south it climbs higher above the horizon.

All that is only part of the story, and only part of the reference to a 'god' which more accurately should have been 'goddess'. Forming part of the southern horizon seen from Callanish there is a formation of hills called Cailleach na Mointeach, which translates as 'The Old Woman of the Moors'. The locals know her as 'Sleeping Beauty'. Those hills clearly and quite breathtakingly form the outline of a woman lying on her back. The formation is a magical phenomenon that no photograph I have ever seen can adequately capture (picture 7 is no exception), and not only at Callanish can this be observed; it is evident at all the neighbouring Neolithic sites. From one of them Sleeping Beauty appears pregnant, with open knees prepared for an imminent birth!

The relationships between all the sites and Sleeping Beauty were discovered by a truly remarkable resident of Lewis named Margaret Curtis. After years of research, Margaret realised that Callanish is aligned on the Southern Major rising and setting of the moon. In June 1987, Margaret watched from the avenue as the moon rose out of the chest of Sleeping Beauty, passed across the eastern avenue of stones, and then dipped behind the rocky outcrop of Cnoc an Tursa before reappearing at the foot of the central stone. Julian Cope reports that Margaret later wrote, "For three minutes, never revealing more than half of its orb in the narrow gap, the moon was captured in the artificial frame of megaliths and the cold grey pillars of stone were bathed in a golden glow. Like a lighthouse beam the moonlight stretched along the avenue towards us and caught us in its light." (Julian Cope *The Modern Antiquarian*, Thorsons 1995.)

To die for! Well, almost. Since the time of the monument's construction, the declination of the Southern Major limit of the moon has changed by 0.55°, and the moon is now a little higher in the sky. Around 2800 BC, it would have risen out of Sleeping

Beauty and its setting would have been captured within the stones, but not for the duration of three minutes. The narrow gap between the central stones frames a distinct notch in the distant skyline that looks very much like a gun-sight fractionally above the Cnoc an Tursa outcrop. It is probable that the only sighting of the setting moon would have been of its upper limb winking its goodbye precisely in the notch, and that Callanish is more accurately aligned on the lunar event than even Margaret Curtis realised.

Picture 7. Sleeping Beauty from Callanish.

When I visited the site in 2006 for the next extreme southerly moon, clouds obscured the reappearance of the moon within the circle. Yet I will never forget seeing it rise out of Sleeping Beauty then appear to roll along her face and onward over the eastern avenue of stones. I know it's a cliché, but you really did need to be there. Even for someone such as myself with no particular religious affiliation, it was a very moving spiritual experience. Yes, I knew exactly when and where the moon would appear if the sky remained clear, although nothing can prepare anyone for those moments when five thousand years-old belief systems are suddenly brought into the present and re-enacted before our eyes. All those years that separate us from the ancient Britons no longer seem to exist, and the effect can only be described as humbling. For an engrossing account of the visionary work of Margaret Curtis and her partner Ron, once again I recommend Julian Cope's *The Modern Antiquarian*.

For Pytheas to have seen Callanish and to have had its usage explained to him, the monument must still have been in use or still clearly understood as late as 330-328 BC. Therefore, despite the possible changes in population and almost certainly in culture that must have occurred during the Bronze and Iron Ages, somehow the Lewis islanders had steadfastly adhered to their ancient ritual practises and belief systems for at least two and a half millennia. At the very least, they must still have respected the old traditions. That does not appear to have been the case elsewhere in the British Isles, where the advent of the Bronze Age brought about many changes. For that reason, the following paragraph is particularly disturbing.

If you have not yet been to Callanish, choose the day of your visit carefully. In 2006, the staunchly Presbyterian islanders of Lewis didn't even bother to open the visitor centre for what is surely the monument's defining event, because it fell on a Sunday. Nor did they provide any security personnel or monitoring of any kind, and a large gang of drunken yobs almost ruined an otherwise wonderful event. I don't know if there is any truth in the rumour that the gang's disruptive behaviour was encouraged by a Christian group, but either way it was not something that the authorities should ever have allowed to happen. Their lack of foresight was tantamount to dereliction of duty, and an insult to the magnificent legacy of their own ancestors. It will come as no surprise therefore, that in 1994, those in charge of Callanish took a JCB and dug a path out of the Cnoc an Tursa outcrop to ease access into the stone circle. Despite the evidence provided by Margaret Curtis, they were oblivious to the fact that the knoll is as integral to the monument as the stones themselves, and they came close to altering the horizon on the crucial alignment.

It was the memory of Sleeping Beauty and the realisation that I had seen vaguely similar hill figures near other prehistoric sites that resonated so strongly in me that November day on Milk Hill when I first became aware of Pecked and Woodborough Hills. It does not take a leap of faith to see the conical Pecked and Silbury Hills as the heads of recumbent figures or 'Sleeping Beauties', with the bodies or pregnant bellies of the Earth Mother represented by Waden and Woodborough Hills. In view of Silbury's archaeological record, and when the hill figures described in part 8 of this book are considered, the only logical conclusion is that Silbury was built for that very purpose.

Picture 8 is Silbury and Waden Hills from the probable stone circle on Harestone Down that was discovered by Terence Meaden and described in his book *Secrets of the Avebury Stones* (Souvenir Press 1999).

There is no longer an adequately clear line of sight to Silbury and Waden Hills from the Sanctuary stone circle. Fortunately, William Stukeley's 18th century illustration (figure 5) clearly depicts their recumbent form. The Winterbourne Bassett stone circle also was ideally placed for visitors to see the recumbent form, but nowadays trees obscure the image, and Stukeley's drawing of the site either did not include Waden Hill, or the drawing's background has faded.

It should be noted that the Winterbourne Basset circle was not located at the scattering of semi-buried sarsen stones that is designated as the site on Ordnance Survey maps at SU 09367752. Those stones and the maps have misled many people over the years, including myself. The perspective of the circle, Silbury Hill and Avebury's church tower as portrayed in Stukeley's drawing shows that the circle's true location was approximately 350 metres away in the field immediately to the south, and close to the road leading to Whyr Farm. Sadly, nothing of it remains to be seen.

Picture 8. Silbury and Waden Hills from Harestone Down.

Figure 5. After Stukeley's illustration of the Sanctuary.

Would these and other hill figures near prehistoric sites necessarily have represented the Earth Mother to the Neolithic people? The only alternative I can think of is that they could have been associated with some form of ancestor 'worship', and possibly represent a shrouded cadaver. Although there is evidence that Neolithic people honoured the memory of their ancestors and kept them close, that is a long way from actually worshipping them, and traditions associated with the hill figures point firmly to the Earth Goddess.

I remember discussing the Silbury enigma with English Heritage's Amanda Chadburn back in around 2003 when she asked "why here?" A very astute question, and one that nobody could answer at the time. Now, Amanda, the answer is that from their causewayed enclosure on Windmill Hill, and indeed from many more of their monuments, the Neolithic people of the Winterbourne/Kennet Valley could see that the natural promontory on which Silbury now stands could be enhanced to work jointly with Waden Hill, and become a most impressive effigy of a recumbent Earth Mother or Goddess. They would have been acutely aware of other Goddess hill figures throughout Britain and perhaps slightly envious of them, especially the one in their very closest neighbours' Vale of Pewsey, which eventually they would copy.

After all, the Kennet Valley people had the largest henge/circle complete with magnificent avenues, the largest hilltop causewayed enclosure and the largest long barrows in the land. Yet they did not have a truly striking landscape figure of their deity in keeping with the grandeur of their monuments. So they built one, and did their utmost to ensure it would last forever. In that context, the existence of Silbury's natural promontory base and its close proximity to Waden Hill is crucial. The mound builders were not inventing anything; they were simply improving what nature had already provided. If that had not been the case, then we could expect to find Silbury-type mounds throughout Britain, and those mounds simply do not exist. Furthermore, the enormity of the undertaking is proof that Silbury was not built to represent a merely local belief system or custom, but something that was universally recognised and celebrated.

In short, Silbury Hill is here because so is Waden Hill. Without Waden, construction of the Silbury mound would not even have been contemplated. The locations of Avebury henge and the West Kennet palisaded enclosures, precisely at the southern and northern ends of Waden Hill's long axis, strongly indicate reverence for the area's original mother landmark. Waden received its current title only around 1,500 years ago when it was named by the incoming Saxons after Woden, the father of their entire pantheon of Gods. It is reasonable to assume they did so because they knew something of the creator traditions associated with the hill. By changing the gender of the matriarchal icon, they incorporated it into their own belief systems.

If the effigy hypothesis is correct, why were Silbury's causeways left intact? It seems incongruous that such a sacred icon would have been walked on or climbed, and yet the causeways indicate that access to the mound was necessary. It is possible they were left in place simply for maintenance purposes, but if Silbury's (probably rounded) summit did indeed present a panorama composed purely of its own water-catchment area from a location at the source of its own river, it would have represented an achievement that no other communities could ever have the chance to emulate. That would have been a very good reason to leave the causeways in place.

The Neolithic date of Marlborough Mount proves that Silbury Hill is not unique. Initially, I was puzzled by the Mount's appearance as the only conical 'head' for which I could not find an accompanying 'body' hill, although the encroachment of Marlborough's buildings renders a clear perspective of the landscape impossible. Unless it had been destroyed by building work or intensive ploughing, which I very much doubted, I thought that Marlborough's body hill was still waiting to be identified. Then, I began to realise the problem may only have been a matter of perspective. I had noticed that many of the conical hills within recumbent figures stood on low ground, or a coll, in between two or more hills. The effect is that the body is seen on both sides of the head. This can be seen at Silbury from various perspectives, and classic natural examples are in the view from Hembury causewayed enclosure and at Corfe Castle. Perhaps Marlborough Mount was intended to be viewed that way, in between the high ground that rises to both the north and south of it.

The Mount stands just upstream of a natural bottleneck in the river valley formed by the spurs of Marlborough Common and Granham Hill. It is also upstream of the River Kennet's first river tributary, namely the River Og. With no further tributaries between the Mount and Silbury, for anyone travelling upstream, the Mount and its spring mark the beginning of the only section of the river that is fed purely by Silbury's environs. Therefore, the Mount and its narrow surroundings between the spurs may have been intended as a ceremonial gateway into the upper reaches of Silbury's revered river valley. Complete with its spring-fed ditch that mirrored Silbury's, the Mount would have served as a foretaste of the greater mound and hill figure that travellers would soon encounter five miles further on at the source of the river.

If that indeed was the intention, Marlborough Mount's builders could not have chosen a more appropriate site. That would explain why the two greatest monumental mounds in Britain are so close to each other and in the same river valley. In addition, the Sanctuary stone circle marks the beginning of Avebury's West Kennet Avenue, and is less than 400m from the river on the ancient track of the Ridgeway. The river route could have diverted at that point to join the megalithic avenue and to follow it into the great Avebury henge. At the point where the river route joined the Ridgeway and the Sanctuary, the recumbent figure formed by Silbury and Waden Hills would have revealed itself as being central to the sacred Avebury landscape, and pilgrims would have known they had arrived in the domain of the Silbury Goddess (take another look at figure 5).

Although Neolithic trackways were much more likely to have been on high ground where there would have been fewer obstructions and better views, there is a very famous precedent for the proposed ceremonial route alongside the River Kennet from the Marlborough Mount to the Avebury complex. The Stonehenge Riverside project has discovered a Neolithic 'road' or avenue of compacted flint that led from the Durrington Walls henge for a short distance to the River Avon. Approximately five miles downstream from Durrington Walls, the Stonehenge avenue also leads from the river to the iconic monument's north-eastern entrance. There can be no doubt the river was used as a link between the living quarters of Durrington Walls and the ceremonial centre of Stonehenge. Located only sixteen miles from Stonehenge, it seems highly likely that the great complex around Avebury and the River Kennet also had a river route.

Owing to their largely natural formation, no two Goddess hill figures are ever exactly the same. Nevertheless, the monuments built into their landscapes, or the folk tales and traditions surrounding them, are very strong evidence that the Neolithic people of Britain saw them all as variations on the same theme. Indeed, there are similar traditions throughout the World, particularly in Europe. Silbury Hill and Marlborough Mount are believed to be the only extant artificial prehistoric hills of any great magnitude in Britain, although I suspect that some of the 'natural' hill figures have received a helping hand, as some of them appear unnaturally stylised.

Not all Neolithic monuments were constructed within sight of a classic 'head and body' hill figure. How could they have been? If a settlement had grown in a location that provided fertile ground and a good water supply, its inhabitants would have made use of whatever dominant home landmark was available to them. I grew up in Clitheroe in the lee of Pendle Hill, one of Lancashire's most memorable landmarks, and infamous for its association with witch persecutions. To this day, despite having moved from the town twenty-five years ago, whenever I see Pendle I invariably have the sense that I am home, and I know that many other people share that experience in their own home areas. I suspect we all do. How much stronger would that sense have been to Neolithic communities with much closer ties to the land than any one of us? Regardless of the shape or form of whichever landmark they dedicated their monuments to, the Neolithic people would always have seen it as representing the bounty of their home ground, and by association, the benevolence of the Earth Mother.

When I first realised the significance of the hill figures, I rather optimistically conjectured there could emerge a particular type of monument from which hill figures are invariably seen, and that ritual practises dedicated to the Earth Mother could then confidently be said to have taken place at all sites of similar design. As yet, that does not seem to be the case, although that is largely owing to the fact that many monuments of very diverse size, design and antiquity are grouped together under the same archaeological classifications. That is particularly true of causewayed enclosures, which can be massive and multi-ringed or appear to amount to little more than the remains of modest livestock pens. Clearly, all those sites were not designed for the same purpose or the same rituals and ceremonies. The absence of suitable radiocarbon dating materials at many sites exacerbates the problem, especially at stone circles, some of which cannot be dated with any accuracy within a thousand years and which display bewilderingly diverse characteristics.

At some time in the future, classification of monuments will undoubtedly become a more exact science. Until then, unless someone undertakes the Herculean task of accurately inspecting the landscape of every known and suspected prehistoric site, whether it is surrounded by trees and buildings or not, all that can be said is that some ancient sites share their landscape with hill figures and some do not. Where they do not, there will be a reason relating either to the age of the site or its original usage. Even so, at the time of writing, it appears that standing stones erected in the centuries around 3000 BC are very likely to be in the domain of an Earth Mother hill figure.

Part 8. Some Pre-Silbury Silburys.

Although it seems most likely that Silbury Hill was modelled on the nearby Pecked Hill, there really is only one candidate for the quintessential 'head and body' hill. The mother of them all has to be Glastonbury Tor. Steeped in religious traditions that date back to the Neolithic period, this unworldly eminence rises 145m out of the Somerset Levels to present one of the most captivating landscape features in Britain. From many perspectives it is unquestionably Silbury-like in appearance, and that is the image presented on all the postcards, calendars and book covers. It is the Isle of Avalon of Arthurian legend, overlooking the Glastonbury Thorn that is said to have grown from a staff planted by Joseph of Arimathea in the presence of a young Christ. Who cares if the stories are untrue? The sheer power of place generated by the Tor demands that if no such legends existed, someone would have to make them up! For the opening ceremony of London's 2012 Olympic Games, out of all the iconic British landmarks that could have been chosen, it was a model of Glastonbury Tor that took the stage.

A number of wooden walkways dating back as far as 3807 BC have been found where they cross the Somerset Levels linking areas of high ground. Although a matter of some quite heated debate, it is likely that the Tor and the other nearby 'islands' were in fact just that during the Neolithic – literally inundated by water from the Bristol Channel. At the very least they would have been surrounded by very marshy ground, and it is known that high seasonal flooding occurred up to the Early Medieval period.

To see the Tor surrounded by water in any age would be a magical experience, and to the Neolithic people it must have appeared like Heaven on Earth. Silbury's builders certainly would have been aware of Glastonbury's renowned beauty and sanctity, and I believe that one of their reasons for surrounding their own great mound with a deep ditch can be attributed to Glastonbury Tor's watery Neolithic environment. It is even possible that Silbury's spiral form or walkway was inspired by a distinctive series of terraces on the Tor's slopes. The purpose and date of the terraces are unknown; it is possible they are remnants of medieval agriculture or cattle grazing, or they could be evidence of a Neolithic labyrinth or spiral walkway. Another theory that they are Iron Age fortifications is clearly misconceived, as they do not consist of banks and ditches, and the 'defended' summit area is far too small. The historian and broadcaster Alistair Moffat has presented a convincing case that so-called Iron Age forts were in fact palaces, constructed and used by ruling elite groups such as druids or by dominant extended families. If correct, the summit area of the Tor would still be too small to have been considered a palace.

There is much more to Glastonbury's Goddess figure than merely the Tor 'head' itself. Remarkably, it does not seem to matter from which direction one observes it. The unique formation of high ground leading up to the Tor always presents an image of an accompanying 'body' to one side or another, as if in a deliberate arrangement (pictures 9 and 10 are two examples). Of course it could not have been so, although it is further evidence that during the Neolithic period certain places were believed to be sacred because of their association with the Earth Mother. That belief, or at least an intuitive memory of it, seems to have endured throughout the ages: for many people, Glastonbury has a magnetic attraction.

Picture 9. Glastonbury Tor.

Picture 10. The Tor from a different perspective.

Is there something deep within people, some kind of collective memory of Neolithic practises and sacred places that keeps us enthralled? Perhaps it is no coincidence that great annual party gatherings still take place at Glastonbury, Stonehenge and Avebury. Try sleeping on Glastonbury Tor, it will awaken spirituality in you that you never knew existed. I can recommend the stone seat in the summit tower that provided one of the most unforgettable nights of my life, but wrap up warmly at any time of year.

Despite having previously completed a survey of all the important solar and lunar alignments in the Stonehenge skyline, I had never noticed anything that could have represented the Earth Mother. It was only recently that I suspected such a thing could have existed. A number of inspections from the monument itself subsequently revealed nothing. Remembering that causewayed enclosures often seem to overlook Earth Mother figures, I went to Stonehenge's neighbouring causewayed enclosure at Robin Hood's Ball. Again, nothing of interest could be seen, but a section of the landscape that was obscured by woods proved to be the key.

As I was about to give up on any appropriate hill figure in the area, I was parking the car back at Stonehenge when I noticed a familiar outline on the horizon between a gap in the trees on King Barrow ridge. It was in the same section of the landscape that is blocked from sight at Robin Hood's Ball. When viewed from King Barrow ridge the figure became obvious, running roughly in a north/south line with the body formed by Beacon Hill. The 'head and face' in picture 11 definitely is not merely a clump of trees; they cover a distinctive knoll known as Clay Mound that rises steeply at least 20m above the coll immediately to its north (left in the picture). At the time of Stonehenge's initial construction *c.*3000 BC, the knoll would have been even more distinctive, as 5,000 years of erosion have conspired to silt up the coll and the gap between Beacon Hill and Clay Mound. Nevertheless, the recumbent form is still clearly visible, and it completely dominates the eastern skyline at Durrington Walls henge and Woodhenge. From Stonehenge, the entire figure would appear to be in repose on King Barrow ridge (picture 12) if it wasn't for those trees! Note the position of the higher communications mast in both pictures.

Picture 11. Clay mound and Beacon Hill from the King Barrow ridge.

Knowledge of Stonehenge and its environs has grown immensely since the Stonehenge Riverside Project began in 2003. Led by Professor Mike Parker Pearson, the project ran for seven years. During that time, forty-five archaeological excavations were

Picture 12. The reason why Clay Mound and Beacon Hill can no longer be seen from Stonehenge.

opened throughout the Stonehenge World Heritage Site's 26.6 square kilometres. One of the most significant findings was the discovery of unusually deep periglacial gullies within the Stonehenge avenue. This ceremonial route comprises of two parallel banks and ditches that run from Stonehenge down to the River Avon. Approximately the first 700m run north-east in a straight line down to lower ground at Stonehenge Bottom, before turning sharply eastward up to King Barrow ridge. The periglacial gullies or 'stripes' run for around 500m within the avenue. The stripes are entirely natural, formed by the flow of meltwater as ice-age glaciers and snowfields retreated.

Apart from the unusual depth of the gullies there is nothing remarkable in all that; such features are found throughout southern England's chalklands. It is only when the precise Summer Solstice sunrise/Winter Solstice sunset alignment of the avenue's initial straight section is considered that the implications become clear. Lying as they do within the avenue, the natural periglacial stripes also must be aligned on the solstices, and therefore must have seemed extremely providential to the builders of Stonehenge. As such, they could very well be the answer (or one of the answers) to the age-old question of why Stonehenge is located where it is. Because of that, if the Riverside Project had made no other discoveries at all, the entire project would still have been worthwhile. However, much more has been revealed, particularly at Durrington Walls. For a comprehensive report of the findings you will need a copy of Parker Pearson's *Stonehenge* (Simon and Schuster 2012), and you will never have spent money more wisely.

Of course, the true significance of the periglacial features depends on whether or not the stripes were discernible under Neolithic soils that were around 30 to 50 centimetres deeper than at present. The silted-up stripes are not visible to the naked eye, and they were only discovered by digging. Then again, there are yet more natural features on the solstice alignments, consisting of three ridges that run for the first 200m of the avenue as it leaves Stonehenge. It was on two of these that the avenue's banks were constructed. The ridges definitely would have been highly visible during the Neolithic period, and owing to subsequent erosion they would have been much more clearly defined than at present. Therefore, visibility of the periglacial stripes may not have been so important in the Neolithic period, although they probably would have been visible as dark stripes during times of drought.

What we can be certain of is that thousands of years earlier in the Mesolithic period, the stripes would have been clearly visible under a thin grass cover and slowly developing soils.

In 1966, the Stonehenge car park was enlarged and an archaeological dig in advance of its construction was undertaken. Three postholes around 0.75m in diameter were discovered. After inspection they were buried beneath the car park (surprising but true), their positions marked by white-painted circles. Quite astonishingly, the two that were tested yielded radiocarbon dates of *c*.8000 BC, although the two dates did not entirely overlap. As Parker Pearson explains in *Stonehenge*, radiocarbon dates were taken from charcoal found within the postholes that came from charred pine-tree trunks. Being 0.75m in diameter, the trees could have accumulated up to three hundred annual growth rings, "so the charcoal could come from rings growing at any point in the tree's life."(Ibid.) Consequently, a slight discrepancy in the two dates is hardly surprising.

Parker Pearson wrote that the postholes and a large tree-hole found next to them run "in an east-west line" (ibid) and the artist's reconstruction in his book clearly depicts all four features in a line.

It can only have been a band of Mesolithic hunters that erected the posts, probably as they revisited a seasonal hunting ground that was well known to them. In reference to the hunters and the seemingly miraculous periglacial stripes feature, Parker Pearson wrote "Around it, they camped, dug pits and erected pine-tree posts, marking the direction of the highest hill on the horizon" (ibid). That is a questionable interpretation, for although they are roughly aligned on the highest ground in the skyline formed by Beacon Hill, the postholes are around 300m from the stripes, and in no way do they share the same alignment. Neither do they actually run in a straight line. If the intention had been to mark the area as special because of the stripes, the hunters could have made that intention much clearer by erecting their posts at each end of the stripes, or at least aligning with them. It is also dubious whether a roving band of hunter-gatherers would recognise the solstice alignments of the stripes in an area where such stripes were commonplace, unless the hunters just happened to be there at the time of the solstices. Even then it must be asked whether they would have been aware of the actual Summer Solstice sunrise and Winter Solstice sunset alignments, which to the naked eye are indistinguishable from the three or four days immediately before and after them. Of course, the hunters may have realised the stripes were aligned in the general direction of the solstices.

Another pit was discovered around 100m to the east of the three postholes, but its clearly defined layers of backfilling indicate it was just a pit and probably never held a post. It is possible there are many more waiting to be discovered, and the three postholes may be part of a larger arrangement that had nothing to do with pointing at the highest ground at all. Nevertheless, their close proximity to each other indicates they were intended to share a certain role, and that they are of much greater significance than previously realised, for only two of them actually point to Beacon Hill's summit.

The postholes definitely are not in a line; there is an obvious 'dog-leg' in their course (picture 13 looking eastward). The eastern and central postholes have a clear line of sight through a gap in the trees and are aligned directly on Clay Mound, as can be seen in the picture. Note also how the whole of the hill figure would have appeared to rest on the nearby King Barrow ridge. Although the central and western postholes do not have a clear line of sight, they align with a point approximately 750m south of Beacon Hill's summit. It would have been a simple matter to erect just the two western and eastern posts to align on the summit if that had been the intention, and the addition of the central post indicates it was not. Why would anyone want to mark high ground in such a way when high ground is its own marker? It appears far more likely that the intention was to align the eastern and central posts with the Clay Mound 'head', the western and eastern posts with the Beacon Hill 'body', and the western and central posts with what may have been perceived as the 'foot' of the hill figure. The sightlines move naturally from the left to the centre, then to the right. Despite millennia of erosion and ploughing to the southern section of the figure's slopes, the position the western and central postholes point to still appears to be the foot or end of the figure in the far right of picture 10. If that hypothesis is correct, the Stonehenge car park covered the earliest monument dedicated to the Earth Mother that has ever been found. Thankfully, with the new visitor centre now complete, the old car park is being returned to landscape.

If the postholes eventually prove not to be contemporaneous, or if they are part of a larger arrangement, their present alignment must be one of the most astonishing coincidences in British archaeology.

If the posts were intended for the proposed purpose, why would hunter-gatherers want to erect them? If the ability to recognise landmarks was important to Neolithic farmers, it would have been even more important to hunters who did not settle for very long in any one place. There is a Mesolithic encampment just over a mile to the east of Stonehenge that has recently yielded evidence of seasonal usage over thousands of years. People visiting the camp must have been aware of the high ground formed by Beacon Hill and Clay Mound, and would have used those hills as a navigation aid. Such a prominent landmark that resembled a recumbent human form would certainly have been worthy of being commemorated by the posts. The posthole alignments can easily be checked by anyone visiting the car park, assuming that tourists' coaches aren't in the way!

Picture 13. The car park postholes. Clearly not in a straight line.

Around 750m north of Stonehenge is a Neolithic earthwork known as the greater cursus. 2.75kms long and running roughly in an east to west line, it consists of two almost parallel banks and ditches that culminate in banks and ditches at either end. Radiocarbon dates indicate it was constructed at some time between 3660 and 3370 BC for purposes totally unknown. From the western end, its southern bank and ditch run in a straight line eastward for about 550m before kinking slightly to the north. In common with the car park postholes, this section is often reported as being aligned on the highest point on the horizon. It is not and was never intended to be. It points directly at a prominent knoll covered in trees at least 500m from Beacon Hill's summit, and Neolithic builders did not make such mistakes. If any significance can be attached to the section, and the deliberate kink in its course indicates that it can, then an obvious conclusion may be drawn, for the "prominent knoll" on which it aligns is none other than Clay Mound.

The discovery of the periglacial stripes and the ridges is certainly highly significant, and it cannot be a coincidence that they point straight at Stonehenge and were incorporated into its avenue. Nevertheless, there will always be those who cannot bring themselves to accept that the stripes could have been a determinant of the monument's location. Many among the alternative community find that too prosaic an explanation, and prefer to adhere to their own arcane beliefs. They argue that the stripes would not have been visible under deep Neolithic soils, which is true, but surely the odds against the monument's accurate alignment with the stripes, ridges and solstices being merely coincidental are so high that any impartial observer can dismiss the possibility out of hand.

The builders of Stonehenge must have known of the stripes' existence; knowledge of them would probably have been handed down from generation to generation since the Mesolithic era. Nevertheless, if the stripes and ridges were the only factors involved in the placement of the monument, their Summer Solstice/Winter Solstice alignment could have been more conspicuously celebrated by placing the monument *within* them. That way, observers inside the monument could have looked along the stripes in both directions to view the solstice alignments. The sloping ground would not have been a deterrent because Stonehenge is built on a slope anyway, and locating the monument on slightly lower ground would not have altered the elevation of the horizon sufficiently to change the solstitial azimuths.

Could the solstitial alignments of the stripes and ridges have been sufficient reason to place such an important monument where it is? It seems more likely that their existence, and the fact they lead to the point where the Earth Mother hill figure would have been seen in sublime repose above King Barrow ridge were the combination of factors that determined our most famous monument's location The alignment of the car park postholes would appear to vindicate that.

There is further evidence that the 'sacred feminine' was very much in the thoughts of the monument builders on Salisbury Plain. Although the Stonehenge axis can be said to be aligned on the solstices and therefore the 'male' energies of the sun, the only stones that are similarly aligned are the four Station Stone settings that were placed just within the monument's ditch and bank. The Station Stones also are aligned with the 'female' moon at its Southern Major rising and Northern Major setting. As previously stated, the famous Heelstone definitely was not aligned with the Summer Solstice sunrise. After it had probably been removed from its original location (the adjacent stone hole 97) during stage two of the monument's construction around 2620-2480 BC, it was then precisely aligned from the centre of the monument on the mid-swing rising of the northern moon as the moon moved between its major and minor extremes. That alignment has 'pride of place' within the entrance arch of the sarsen circle, which was erected during the same period.

Although that has been documented previously, another lunar alignment has largely been overlooked. Again, from the centre of Stonehenge, the Coneybury Hill tumulus is seen to stand proudly on the south-eastern horizon, where it marked the rising of the Southern Minor Moon around 2500 BC. Proof that the alignment is not merely a coincidence can be found at the centre of Woodhenge, from where the very same tumulus forms a narrow section of the horizon, and marked the setting of the Southern Major Moon. That alignment could be the reason why Woodhenge is so close and yet so strangely isolated from the adjacent Durrington Walls henge. The henge and all the timber circles within it stood on much lower ground, from where the moon could only be seen to set on the henge bank, not the true horizon. If the Coneybury tumulus did not exist in the period of usage of Stonehenge and Woodhenge (I can find no references to its date), its lunar alignments clearly indicate that something of significance must have stood in the same location.

In 2001, Joshua Pollard and Clive Ruggles published the paper *Shifting Perceptions* (Cambridge Archaeological Journal 11.1. 2001 pp 69-90), in which they analysed deposits of cremations, human bones, animal bones, antlers, worked chalk and flints in the Stonehenge ditch. They found "It is perhaps of significance that those deposits most closely allied to the motions of the moon are of human bone (principally cremations.)" (Ibid.) They also wrote that Neolithic people appeared to have demonstrated a "sustained interest in the narrow sector of the enclosure perimeter between azimuths 134° and 142°, and its apparent relationship with a specific lunar event – the rising of the midsummer full moon." The authors concluded "cremations and other deposits were placed in relation to the rising moon at propitious times." (Ibid.)

If the setting Winter Solstice sun was meant to be viewed within the narrow gap between the uprights of Stonehenge's Great Trilithon (and every account you can read claims that it was), why was the tallest stone of the bluestone oval subsequently placed directly in front of the gap, completely blocking the view of the sunset? Although the bluestone is now fallen, why do most writers and documentary presenters seem to develop amnesia about its original setting? The quite deliberate placement of that bluestone looks very much like a statement of intent, and Stonehenge's purported relationship with the sun may have been unwittingly overstated.

General reluctance to address the question of the bluestone oval appears to have no end. A video presentation at the new Stonehenge visitor centre clumsily avoids the issue by portraying the oval as being about knee-high, whereas the stones actually were around 2m tall. It is reminiscent of a scene in the spoof rock-documentary *This is Spinal Tap* when a member of the hapless rock-band produces a drawing of a stage prop in the form of Stonehenge's Great Trilithon. The drawing's measurements are mistakenly marked in the symbol for imperial inches instead of feet, resulting in a ludicrously small stage prop. In an attempt to balance perspective of the mini-trilithon, the tour manager hires two dwarves to dance around it. Of course, the effect is hilarious and the band are publicly humiliated. If English Heritage insist on miniaturising the bluestones in the video presentation, then why not show dwarves dancing around them? That would be much more entertaining and informative.

Pottery known as Grooved Ware is common at Neolithic sites throughout Britain, and the style was adopted around 2800 BC in the Stonehenge area. At least four hundred years earlier it was being made in the islands of Orkney, from where Britain's Neolithic religious and cultural practises seem to have spread. The islands have an astonishingly well-preserved array of monuments and settlements that date back to hundreds of years before 3000 BC. Among the most impressive of them are found on mainland Orkney, clustered around a narrow isthmus of land at the Ness of Brodgar. At the time of writing, a temple complex larger than any previously found in Europe is under excavation there, alongside the famous Ring of Brodgar, the Stones of Stennes, Neolithic settlements and individual standing stones. All those sites are overlooked by a captivating hill formation on the neighbouring island of Hoy that towers above intervening ground.

Close to the Ness is one of Europe's finest examples of a chambered cairn known as Maes Howe. It was constructed with precisely cut stones that fitted together without any form of bonding, and originally it was capped with a corbelled roof that required consummate skill to erect. Sadly, the roof was destroyed by marauding Vikings and has now been replaced by a Victorian construction. The enormous passage mound is aligned towards the setting midwinter sun. For around three weeks before and after the Winter Solstice, the setting sun shines directly down the passageway to illuminate the back wall of the spacious main chamber, and sets within the same hill formation that overlooks the Ness of Brodgar. The significance of the shape of those hills is quite obvious when viewed from the Maes Howe entrance, and surely must have strong implications for later constructions elsewhere.

The setting Winter Solstice sun denotes the death of the year, and heralds its rebirth with lengthening days to come. By locating and aligning Maes Howe the way they did, the Neolithic people of Orkney could witness the sunsets of the propitious winter event, the days leading up to it and the early days of the new year all being captured within their recumbent Earth Mother hill figure. Simultaneously, the sun's rays were enshrined deep inside their magnificent chamber. Therefore, the archaeological interpretation of Maes Howe as being merely a house of the dead is patently unsatisfactory. Clearly, rebirth and the cyclical order of Mother Nature were in the minds of its constructors.

Incidentally, there is a 'dog-leg' in the course of Maes Howe's passageway that has no official explanation. The function of the passageway must have been to allow access into the chamber, and therefore it had to be wide enough for people to pass through. If its width was considered to have allowed too wide a beam of light to illuminate the inner chamber's back wall, thereby failing to focus on a specific and designated part of the wall on any given day, then the dog-leg would narrow the beam and still allow access to people.

At a very recent lecture given by Professor Mike Parker Pearson (Nov 2013), that most erudite of gentlemen recounted a conversation between himself and other archaeologists in which they discussed the temple complex currently being excavated at the Ness of Brodgar. None of them had suspected any such monument could ever have existed in that particular location. One of the group mentioned he had been informed by a local guide that, from the site of the temple, the Winter Solstice sun is seen to set exactly in between the two hills on Hoy. At the lecture, Parker Pearson speculated that as we rediscover the importance of such sightlines to Neolithic people "At some time in the future it may lead us to understand their religion."

We're already there professor; those are no ordinary hills on Hoy.

Pictures 14. Looking out from Maes Howe's entrance.

Picture 15. Taken from the same location.

On 30th December 2013, the historian Neil Oliver presented the first episode of BBC 2's *The Sacred Wonders of Britain.* He travelled to Orkney where he examined the stones of the Ring of Brodgar. Evidently, all the stones of this great henge monument are of different sizes and shapes, and geologically they appear to have been gathered from various parts of the Orkney mainland. Oliver suggested this was evidence of a desire to form one large social group from multiple communities scattered around the island, and as the Orkney monuments are amongst the earliest in Britain, this exercise in social bonding could have been the inspiration for subsequent megalithic constructions throughout Britain. That has the ring of truth about it, and is reminiscent of another lecture given by Parker Pearson in which he suggested that the unique architecture of Stonehenge, and the fact that people from throughout Britain gathered there, was evidence of an attempt to bond the entire nation.

Moving on to the temple complex at the Ness of Brodgar, Neil Oliver noted the diversity of design within the dozen or so buildings within the complex, and pondered whether that also was evidence of the contributions of various communities brought together in a common purpose. As he interviewed the team leader of the temple excavators, they discussed the location of the temple and whether that had any religious connotations. The solstitial orientation of some of the buildings was mentioned, and Oliver wondered if their orientation and location could be indicators of the origin of Neolithic religious practises. It is appropriate that the programme was first aired during the pantomime season, for during his conversation with the lead excavator inside the temple, the hills of Hoy were clearly visible in the background. All together now, "She's behind you!"

One of the most striking examples of an Earth Mother hill figure is found at Mere, Wiltshire. It is one that I suspect was partly shaped by human hand. The head is formed by Mere Castle Hill and the body by Long Hill, both standing directly below Whitesheet Hill's Neolithic causewayed enclosure. Castle Hill was truncated in 1253 when the Earl of Cornwall built his castle, of which nothing now remains. Picture 16 taken from the causewayed enclosure shows the hill topped by a flagpole, with the elegant wooded form of Long Hill alongside. To my eye, Long Hill looks just a little too elegant to be entirely natural.

Picture 16. Castle and Long Hills from the Whitesheet enclosures.

In the middle distance another hill formation that looks very much like a recumbent figure can be seen. Picture 17 shows how this one appears from the Hambledon Hill causewayed enclosures approximately fifteen miles south of Whitesheet Hill.

Prominent above the eponymously named town of Bridport on the Dorset coast is another Earth Mother hill figure with a head formed by Colmer's Hill (picture 18). According to Julian Cope, this is "the land of Bridgit or Bride." (Ibid.) It is certainly an area richly endowed with place names linked to the ancient British deity, with Bridport itself, Littlebredy, Long Bredy and the Rivers Bride and Brit.

Just over three miles from Bridport centre stands the famous landmark of Golden Cap. It forms the highest point on the South Coast of England, and its Earth Mother outline is breathtaking (picture 19). No surprise then, that West Dorset's oldest human settlement has been found on the next headland on Doghouse Hill, which is overlooked by Golden Cap. Recent finds indicate human habitation from the Mesolithic period right through to the Bronze Age, and that did not happen simply because the headlands form part of the coastline. We could expect to find ancient human settlements on the coast where seafood would have been abundant, but even as late as the Bronze Age both Golden Cap and Doghouse Hill would have been over a mile inland, and probably over two miles in the Neolithic period. Sadly, if coastal erosion continues at that rate, it may not be very far into the future that Golden Cap is washed away. Its composition of a yellow capping of weathered Upper Greensand over lower Jurassic Liassic clays will probably not be robust enough to resist wind, rain and tide.

Picture 17. From Hambledon Hill.

Picture 18. Colmer's Hill above Bridport.

Picture 19. Golden Cap.

Cley Hill near Longleat in Wiltshire (picture 20) is "a magnificent sacred hill loudly declaring itself to one and all" (Julian Cope, ibid). It is reputed to be home to the king of Wiltshire's fairies, and there are the usual legends attached to such imposing landmarks regarding the Devil etc, although there is no evidence of any Neolithic activity in its immediate surroundings. However, the fact that such a prominent hill with glorious views and an eminently suitable summit area never had a Neolithic monument of any kind indicates that it would have been deemed special or sacred. That is typical of all but one of the proposed Mother hills in this book. It was only much later in the Iron Age that any of the Mother hills were interfered with in that manner, in a time that possibly witnessed the last rites of the Earth Goddess culture.

Picture 20. Cley Hill.

From around 2500 BC, pottery in the 'Beaker' style began spreading throughout Britain, and within one hundred years or less it appears to have become well established. Although it may simply have been a new fashion, its appearance coincides with what seem to have been certain changes in ritual practises, and in some cases changes to monuments (the new radiocarbon dates described in part 6 show this period to be contemporary with Silbury Hill). It is thought the style was introduced by an unknown number of 'Beaker People' who came in from Europe and brought extensive knowledge of metalworking with them. It is still debatable whether there was large-scale immigration or not, but whatever the number of newcomers, they or their innovative ideas seem to have effected British religion and culture. People burrowed deep to find the new precious ores, and it is possible that within some communities reverence for a past provider that had always hidden such a profitable and practical resource would have been on the wane. Alternatively, metalworking could have heralded resurgence in reverence for the Earth Mother, and Silbury Hill could be evidence of that.

One possible exception to the Neolithic people's apparent reluctance to construct monuments or settlements on their sacred hills can be found at the most revered and one of the most strikingly prominent hills in Cornwall. Beacon fire ceremonies dating back to pagan times still take place on Carn Brae's summit on Midsummer Eve, and Christian services are held at Easter. The castle on the hilltop originated as a chapel in 1379, and a plaque at St. Euny's well at the foot of the Carn commemorates a visit by the Celtic missionary in the year 500. A Celtic cross 27m in height was erected on its summit in 1836. The old Cornish name Carn Brae seems evocative of the 'Bridgit' theme once again, and there was certainly a Neolithic enclosure at the site that could date back as far as 3700 BC.

In common with other enclosures at Gloucestershire's Crickley Hill and Dorset's Hambledon Hill, Carn Brae may have been the scene of violent attacks. Masses of flint arrowheads have been found at these sites, along with the remains of wooden buildings destroyed by fire. This has led archaeologists to conclude that violence was the result of territorial disputes, although there is something incongruous about such events occurring in the mid 4th millennium BC when Britain was sparsely populated. There have been many estimates that the total population of mainland Britain at the time numbered only in the tens of thousands, and in his book *Britain BC* (Harper Collins 2003) Francis Pryor estimated a maximum population of one hundred thousand. With such a small population, there must have been plenty of unsettled land to share.

Accounts of the 'attacks' have not placed any significance on the sheer quantity of arrowheads found at the sites (over 750 at Carn Brae). That is a surprising amount of shots to have missed their targets considering that Neolithic raiding parties would not have been more than a few dozen strong at the very most. Either the attackers were very poor marksmen, which is doubtful considering their hunting expertise, or the evidence may have been misinterpreted. Arrow making is a highly skilled and time-consuming process, and most of that time is spent making the shafts. Therefore, it is strange the arrows were not retrieved by either the attackers or the defenders. The pulling of an arrow out of the ground by anyone who understood its construction would not leave the arrowhead behind, and it would not take very long for the wooden shafts to rot away leaving only the flint heads. It is possible that arrows were fired into the air and then deliberately left where they fell during ritualistic, periodic closures of the sites. When Mike Pitts excavated the Sanctuary stone and timber circle at Avebury, he found that timber posts had been consistently burned and re-erected in what he believed to represent the 'coming of age' rituals of successive generations. Avebury's Windmill Hill causewayed enclosures provide further evidence of events in which arrows were used. Enormous quantities of flint arrowheads have been collected from the hill's southern slopes, and those arrowheads are of different ages. They must have accumulated there from activities taking place on a number of separate occasions. "Whatever this activity was, it was one that endured, or at least recurred intermittently." (Leary and Field, ibid.) Burned Neolithic buildings and arrowheads in the ground do not necessarily denote hostility.

There is another possibility that is invariably overlooked in archaeological reports and books on prehistory. Britain's early megalithic culture followed the 'Neolithic Revolution' when previously nomadic groups became farmers. Some people embrace change while others resist it, and simply because certain groups settled down and thereby claimed areas as their own does not mean that everyone did. That would certainly have led to resentment and possibly even conflict when land that had previously been accessible to hunter-gatherers became out of bounds. Agriculture would have disrupted the migration patterns of game animals, which again would have been very inconvenient to those who chose to retain their more unconfined lifestyles. I can fully sympathise with them. If there was indeed violence at Carn Brae and the other hill settlements, it seems far more likely to me that it would have been the result of conflict between ideologies, rather than territorial disputes in the usual sense.

It is possible that Carn Brae was never considered to be an Earth Mother hill, but its name, enduring religious traditions, shape and very powerful presence indicate that it would have been. As such, its Neolithic enclosure could be the exception that proves the rule of mother hills.

Picture 21. Carn Brae's silhouette dominates the skyline above Redruth.

The late psychologist Erich Neumann, the archaeologist Marija Gimbutas and the author Michael Dames have all postulated there is evidence in prehistoric artefacts that the Great Goddess was perceived as having dual sexuality. Phallic symbols and even beards have been found on Goddess figurines and other prehistoric art, suggesting that sexual harmony was perceived as being integral to the harmony and fertility of nature. In *The Silbury Treasure* Dames wrote, "if the divinity was universal, it could not be sexually exclusive." There is evidence for this androgynous understanding of the Goddess at the Hurlers triple stone circle on Bodmin Moor. Aubrey Burl has written that few sites are so important, yet very little significance has been placed on the close proximity of the monument to one of the most remarkable rock formations in England. The Cheesewring (picture 22) caps a natural granite tor, and is the very impressive result of weathering that left multiple discs of stone stacked one over another. It was certainly in place when the Hurlers were erected, and is arguably the reason for their location. Picture 23 was taken from the Hurlers, where the Cheesewring male 'appendage' is conspicuous on another Earth Mother hill figure. Although the figure has been quite shockingly damaged by quarrying, its original profile is still discernible.

Picture 22. The Cheesewring.

Picture 23. The damaged hill figure and The Cheesewring viewed from The Hurlers.

Picture 24. Brentor.

In the 365 square miles of Dartmoor there are the remains of no fewer than 70 stone circles, some of which are accompanied by single, double and even triple rows of stones up to a mile in length. That is a remarkable tally for such a small area (less than 20 x 20 miles), and clearly Dartmoor must have held some special attraction for the monument builders. Unfortunately, "the almost complete absence of C-14 assays and dateable artefacts leaves the chronology of Dartmoor rings in limbo."(Aubrey Burl, *The Stone Circles of Britain Ireland and Brittany,* Yale University Press 2000.) Some are believed to date to around 2800 BC while others could be as late as 1700 BC. Standing proudly on the western edge of Dartmoor is the Glastonbury Tor/Silbury-like eminence of Brentor (picture 24) which is visible from vast swathes of the moor, but I believe it was the topography of the moor itself that inspired the construction of so many ritual sites. Everywhere one looks there are rolling 'body' hills, and 'heads' formed by a myriad of tor peaks. Some are extremely large and high (picture 25), and in close-up even appear to have faces (picture 26), although I am aware that particular observation sounds suspiciously like Christ's image found on a slice of toast, or the Virgin Mary's in a cloud.

Picture 25. A Dartmoor hill figure.

Picture 26. Zoomed in on the 'face'.

One of the most telling sites can be found at a more modest landscape feature of the moor on Down Tor. Picture 27 shows the tor and its very well preserved stone circle and single row. The terminal stone stands at right angles to the row, emphasising the fact that it was placed at the optimum position for an observer to view the outline of the hill figure. If the row had been longer, and the hill figure therefore viewed from a greater distance, its outline would be disrupted by distant hills. If the row had been shorter, the closer perspective would result in the disappearance of the 'feet'. Thousands of years of erosion have undoubtedly taken their toll on the head of the figure, which must have looked even more impressive at the time of the monument's construction. Note in picture 28 how the circle was constructed not on the body hill itself, which would have been disrespectful, but on a flat area at its baseline.

Picture 27. Down Tor.

Picture 28. A closer look at Down Tor's stone circle.

In mountainous Cumbria, it is only to be expected that prehistoric monuments should be located within sight of hill configurations that could be interpreted as Earth Mother figures. There are so many possibilities here it is often difficult to know which, or indeed if any of the figures were perceived that way by the Neolithic people. That is particularly true of the better known stone circles such as Castlerigg near Keswick and Long Meg and her Daughters near Penrith. Castlerigg is completely encircled by spectacular mountains of various shapes and sizes, within which there are at least five possible Earth Mother figures. Unfortunately, not one of them is any more convincing than the others. At Long Meg's circle, there are again five or possibly six potential candidates spread out along the southern horizon, but again none of them actually seems obvious. At two sites in the western Lake District, there is much stronger evidence of Earth Mother homage.

At the Giant's Grave near Millom on the coast, two tall stones stand in view of a hill figure that rivals the majesty of the Sleeping Beauty of Callanish. Formed by the Lakeland fell of Black Combe (picture 29), the figure has a head, a face, an arm by her side, a huge pregnant belly, knees and feet! It is believed this figure was once surrounded by up to six more megalithic sites, rendering it an extremely important ritual centre. Apart from the Giant's Grave, all the sites have now been destroyed. (I know that the Black Combe hill figure has already been documented and photographed from the same perspective by Julian Cope, but I find it so fascinating I just cannot leave it out.)

A little further inland at Swinside stone circle, fifty-five of the possible original sixty stones are still in place, and so are the entrance stones. Once again, it would have been difficult to identify the appropriate hill figure if it was not for the fact the circle's orientation does that for us. Picture 30 shows the entrance aligned on one hill figure, while picture 31 shows another that the entrance stones point to in the opposite direction.

Picture 29. Black Combe from the Giant's Grave.

Picture 30. Swinside circle entrance aligned on a hill figure.

Picture 31. Looking in the opposite direction from Swinside's entrance stones.

The final word on Cumbria must go to its most remarkable and now sadly lost monument. Motorists travelling along the A6 just south of Shap may catch sight of a group of large boulders alongside a railway embankment that runs parallel with the eastern side of the road. The boulders are the remains of the Kemp Howe stone circle that was destroyed when the railway was run straight through it in 1844. The stones have a reddish hue; an attractive characteristic of the local Shap granite, and quite astonishingly they mark the southern terminus of a stone avenue that ran for around 3.5 kms to the north-northwest. In the 16th century, the antiquary William Camden described the avenue stones as being in the form of pyramids, some of which stood "9 feet high and 14 feet thick".

There are conflicting reports of the avenue; some state there were actually two, and there appears to be confusion as to the location of the northern terminus. Most accounts concur that it ended somewhere to the north of an enormous glacial erratic known as the Thunder Stone. Aubrey Burl has estimated around 500 stones in the original avenue rows, while there may have been many more in accompanying circles. Only one still appears to be standing (the Goggleby Stone). Others can be seen lying in the fields, and many more within field walls and the foundations of houses. Destruction of the avenue is believed to have commenced in earnest around 1777, although it is likely that some stones were taken before then.

Along its course, the avenue is reported to have passed through another stone circle that stood slightly to the north of the Greyhound Hotel, probably around 1.25 kms from the avenue's starting point. From there, it continued north-northwest to encircle the Goggleby Stone. Further on, the avenue skirted a once magnificent chambered cairn known as the Skellow Hill Barrow or the 'Hill of Skulls'. The huge barrow was destroyed at the beginning of the 19th century, and subsequent ploughing has reduced it to nothing more than a slight raise in a field. If the monuments had been allowed to survive in anything like their original form, Shap would be the proud home of a monumental landscape rivalling Avebury's, and revenues from tourism would be pouring into a town that looks to be in dire need of them. What a sad and unnecessary loss that truly was.

In keeping with such a stupendous ritual complex, I expected to find a truly remarkable natural landmark in the area, and I was not to be disappointed. At the Kemp Howe circle, a pinnacle on the skyline to the west catches the eye. It is by far the most striking feature of the entire horizon, and it is formed by the unmistakable Lakeland peak of Kidsty Pike. It appears as the 'nose' on a clearly defined 'head', and is accompanied by a 'pregnant belly' hill to its south. As one proceeds along the course of the former avenue, at a point equating to the approximate position of the stone circle reported to have stood north of the Greyhound Hotel, the hill figure becomes complete with 'feet'. At the Goggleby Stone, which stood inside the avenue's rows but was not part of them, the whole hill figure is cradled by a closer ridge (picture 32). This is the finest aspect of the figure, and the Goggleby Stone (extreme right in the picture) appears to have been placed there to mark it.

From there, the figure is visible almost all the way along the avenue's course until its perspective begins to be lost at a point around 1.5 kms north of the Thunder Stone.

Picture 32. Kidsty Pike and the Goggleby Stone.

Picture 33. The figure viewed from the Hill of Skulls.

The new suburban area of Glenrothes in Fife was formerly one of the oldest ceremonial and ritual centres in Britain. It included two henges, two stone circles, a mortuary enclosure, cairns and cists. Dating from around 3200 BC, the sites were in use and occasionally being modified for a period of about 2,000 years. The Balfarg henge still exists in a recognisable form, but it is completely surrounded by a housing development and trees. Only 300m away on the opposite side of the A92, the impressive appearance of the Balbirnie circle disguises the fact that it was moved about 110m to the south-east in 1970 when the road was widened. Its present site also is in the midst of houses and trees with no views of its wider environs. On the subject of Balfarg, Aubrey Burl has written "To visit it and the nearby pleasure of Balbirnie is a megalithic imperative." (*A Guide to the Stone Circles of Britain, Ireland and Brittany*, Yale University Press 1995.) I understand why an area of such antiquity and importance should be visited, but the henge has only two megaliths left in it, and my pleasure in visiting Balbirnie was somewhat tempered by its present position. Location and panorama are crucial to the meaning and usage of all Neolithic monuments, and relocation by 110m can be more than enough to nullify perspective and meaning completely. Even so, I suppose we should be grateful that the monument wasn't simply demolished, with a few token items placed in some local museum.

A little to the east of the two sites there is high open ground with a most convenient lane leading to it. From there, the reason for the location of Balfarg, Balbirnie and the other sites that once accompanied them in their closely spaced ritual complex is revealed. Picture 34 shows the two remarkable eminences of East and West Lomond Hills, and in the foreground, a section of a wooded area immediately to the east of the ritual complex. Although it is difficult to envision a classic Earth Mother figure in the hills, they would have appeared differently from the lower ground of the ritual sites. From there, the skyline ridge between the peaks would be higher, and the two Silbury-like hills could very well have been seen in a more enlightening perspective. Regardless of that, there can be little doubt they are the landscape features that dictated the monuments' locations.

Picture 34. East and west Lomond Hills.

Aberdeenshire is the heartland of Britain's Earth Mother culture. Over 150 stone circles once existed there, and at least 90 are still recognisable. The vast majority of them are of the recumbent stone type that appears to be unique to northeastern Scotland. All these circles have a large level stone lying flat, with the two tallest stones of the circle placed at each side of it to create the impression of horns. At some sites great care was taken to lay the recumbent stone perfectly horizontally, and although the alignments are not always precise, the stone would have appeared as an altar that captured the rising or setting moon. Allegiance to the Earth Mother is most obvious in the area around the Silbury-like eminence of Dunnideer Hill. Standing at the eastern end of a triple hill configuration with Hill of Christ's Kirk and Hill of Flinder, Dunnideer's sacred reputation could hark back to the Neolithic obsession with triplicity, which endured into much later 'Celtic' times. "The Celts were fascinated by triplicity: for example, their gods often took three forms, suffered a triple death or had three characteristics." (Alistair Moffat, *Before Scotland,* Thames and Hudson 2005.) That sounds very much like the Neolithic Great Goddess as Maiden, Mother and Crone.

Julian Cope has written "The sacred omphalos of all Aberdeenshire is the magical hill known as Dunnideer" (ibid), but there are two much more imposing hills in the area, and the clue to their Earth Mother association echoes down in their names. "On either side of the Dunnideer scenery stand two stupendous holy hills. Tap O'Noth, 'the Northern tit'… (and)… Mither Tap or 'Mother Tit' " (Julian Cope, ibid.)

On my one and only whistle-stop tour of Aberdeenshire, I spent the first night in Inverurie having failed to find accommodation of any kind. A two-seater car is not the most comfortable place to sleep, and it was with bleary eyes and a distinct lack of enthusiasm that I perused my map in the morning, wondering where on Earth I should start in the midst of such a proliferation of monuments. The close proximity of Easter Aquhorthies recumbent stone circle seemed convenient, and I had read Aubrey Burl's description that it is a beautiful site to visit. Fifteen minutes later I was there, looking at the brooding summit of Mither Tap. The recumbent stone and its flankers point directly at the hilltop, and although from this perspective the hill does not appear to form an Earth Mother figure in the classic sense, there is no doubt the circle was erected here because of the great hill's presence. Note how in picture 35 the western flanking stone seems to mimic the hill summit. I have often been told that stones in other circles are similarly shaped in order to reflect their surroundings, but I have never seen it to such good effect elsewhere. I stood and stared for quite some time, wondering whether this was a deliberate fashioning of the stone, evidence that the stone had been chosen because of its shape, or simply coincidence. However, after a most inauspicious start, I was beginning to have a very good day.

Picture 35. Mither Tap from Easter Aquhorthies.

Only five miles to the north of Easter Aquhorthies is the famous stone circle known as Loanhead of Daviot, described by Aubrey Burl as one of the most informative of recumbent stone circles. It probably dates to the centuries just after 3000 BC. Owing to nearby trees that block the views to the south and east, I could see nothing of the landscape that inspired its location from within the circle itself. A few paces back towards the car park were necessary to reveal the monument's true focus. Picture 36 is Mither Tap once more.

From Loanhead it is only around ten miles to Dunnideer itself, but time was pressing and there wasn't really anything I could add to Julian Cope's description of the area. I drove through it though, and noted the powerful presence of Tap O'Noth that even the mist in picture 37 cannot hide.

Picture 36. Mither Tap from Loanhead.

After spending only one morning in Aberdeenshire's multitude of stone circles, I had seen enough to convince even the most myopic observer that the landscape of this region inspired the construction of so many monuments. Not even Dartmoor can match it.

Before closing the Aberdeenshire section, I cannot resist including another picture of Mither Tap (38) taken from the north. I do not know of any stone circles in the immediate vicinity, but I would bet the ranch there used to be at least one.

Satisfied as I was with my brief sojourn in the Goddess heartland, I decided to head over to the west coast and visit the Neolithic complex at Kilmartin Glen, south of Oban. In the glen and on its hillsides are stone circles, chambered cairns, cup and ring-marked rocks and much more. An information board outside Kilmartin's museum claims 800 monuments of various types and ages within the glen's seven-mile range, and its Neolithic constructions are amongst the oldest in Britain, dating back as far as 3500 BC. Alas, my good day was about to end as I ran headlong into low cloud and incessant rain, with a forecast that promised little change for three days. If you are reading this, you will know that I have not yet had the chance to return, and the very special Earth Mother figure that is surely there still awaits rediscovery.

Picture 37. Tap O'Noth.

Picture 38.

CONCLUSION

It was the flat tops of the great Silbury monumental mound and its neighbour the Marlborough Mount that had us all fooled for so long. Despite the known modifications to Silbury's original form, which were probably carried out in Saxon times, generations of researchers have believed the summit platform to be at (or very close to) the original height of the monument. The recent confirmation of Professor Richard Atkinson's suggestion that Neolithic revetment walls on top of the mound have been substantially cut in height has led the archaeologists Jim Leary and David Field to surmise that the original summit may have been higher and rounded. Previously, I was convinced along with practically everyone else that the truncated form of the mound and the possibility of a spiral walkway on its slopes meant that Silbury Hill was an observation platform; something that people would have climbed and looked out *from*. That belief motivated my research into the mound's visible horizons and its water-catchment area, and there could still be an element of truth in those findings depending on how much extra height the rounded summit would have created. In addition, the extant causeways indicate the mound was perhaps more than iconic.

The key to understanding the great monumental mound is only found when the hill configuration of Silbury and Waden Hills is compared with Pecked and Woodborough Hills, and with many other hill figures throughout Britain. Leary and Field are right to say that Silbury's original summit was rounded, for Silbury Hill is a replica of Pecked Hill, which has a rounded top. Silbury may have had a secondary role as an observatory with regard to its water-catchment area and therefore its natural domain, but primarily, it was designed to be looked *at*.

Now that it can be stated with certainty that Silbury is not a tomb, if we consider its archaeological record, it seems obvious that to its creators the mound was principally an effigy, for it cannot be anything else. That explains why it is so unlike any other Neolithic monument apart from its Marlborough Mount partner. Silbury appears to be the head of a hill figure, the body of which is formed by Waden Hill. The overall figure can be said to resemble hill figures that are prominent in the landscapes of other Neolithic sites. Those figures appear to be recumbent heads and pregnant bodies, at least four of which still retain their Celtic female names. That strongly indicates an association with a Mother Nature deity; the Great Goddess. The effigy hypothesis would also explain the form and the close proximity to Silbury of the Marlborough Mount, for which no other reasonable explanation has ever been offered.

Silbury Hill is an effigy. Michael Dames pointed us in the right direction way back in 1974 when he declared that Europe's greatest prehistoric mound was a symbol of the Neolithic Earth Mother deity, he just didn't realise how literal a symbol it was. The archaeological community never accepted his hypothesis, mainly because they misunderstood the hydrology of the monument's environs. Now that Late Neolithic water-table levels are believed to have been generally two metres higher than at present, and owing to Steve Marshall's astonishing findings that Silbury's immediate surroundings were a hotbed of springs, all the theories that the mound is a fertility symbol are proven accurate. The River Cunnit rose in a strikingly sacred place that undoubtedly had female connotations.

That is not a romantic interpretation; it is the result of years of research into archaeology and landscape, and the extreme good fortune to have been in the right place at the right time one day in 2010. The Great Goddess or Earth Mother could not have been further from my thoughts when I began my research: I had always believed that Silbury Hill would prove to have a more practical, forgotten function, and that cost me a lot of time. Perhaps initially I could have been more receptive to alternative beliefs, and curbed my natural inclination towards archaeology. Nevertheless, no investigation is complete without every avenue being explored, and if I had to start again, I would probably go about it in the same way.

For those who find the concept of Earth Mother hill figures difficult to accept, first learn to think Neolithic. Contemplate how the bounteous earth would have influenced the beliefs of early hunter-gatherers and Neolithic farmers. Take a long look at the landscapes of Neolithic monuments, and try to imagine the significance that would have been attached to hill figures rising out of the very ground that gave sustenance to the people. I wrote earlier there is a sense of recognition when one looks at the hill figures. That was not entirely accurate; the sense is more like a reawakening of long-dormant beliefs, and it becomes ever more enthralling, as you may have gathered from these pages. I promise it will not be long before you find yourself looking at prehistoric landscapes in an entirely new manner, and when you find one of these hill figures, you will know the truth of it. There are many more of them than I have been able to include in this work, so perhaps I will see you out there exploring one of our sacred landscapes.

Picture 39.

Although her days have gone, the Earth Mother has not been completely forgotten. On the Hebridean island of Harris where the Sleeping Beauty of Callanish actually rises, there is another hill on which a local artist has erected a cairn to mark the navel of a hill figure. The figure is located near Two Waters in the awesome 'moonscape' of South Harris (picture 39). Although the cairn can only be seen by those who climb to the top of the hill, the fact it is there proves that the tradition of recognising the Goddess in the landscape has never died. It never will, "Though out of sight and uncelebrated for millennia, The Great Goddess was too fundamental to culture to ever truly die." (Julian Cope - who else? Ibid.)

The Great Goddess was revered by all Britons for at least a thousand years, and probably much longer. Megalithic structures erected during her heyday incorporated solar and lunar alignments that have been rediscovered in recent times, but foremost, it was to the Goddess herself that Neolithic stone monuments were dedicated. The solar and lunar alignments were only intended to interact with the Earth Mother and to fertilise her. That knowledge has been deliberately erased from history by later religions in a process that may have commenced as early as the Late Neolithic/Early Bronze Age when people from the East brought knowledge of metalworking and subsequently an economy that required dominion of the land, rather than reverence for it.

If Silbury Hill was constructed around 2400 BC as we are now being told, the mound could represent the last flowering of a culture that once held sway throughout Europe. Moreover, if that date is correct, it could indicate that Europe's greatest monumental mound was built to commemorate a deity and a philosophy that had served the people very well for countless generations, even though they accepted that change was inevitable. It could even have been an act of sheer obstinacy, for the Bronze Age came late to Britain compared to the rest of Europe, and it appears the British people were somewhat reluctant to let go of their old ways and customs. Mike Parker Pearson has compared their apparent attitudes to "A Stone Age UKIP!" Of course, the date of Silbury Hill also could represent a time when the Earth Goddess culture simply evolved and became even more monumentalised.

If Silbury Hill was indeed commemorative, its location within the heart of a Neolithic complex such as Avebury's is where we could expect to find it; in one of the last bastions of Europe's Goddess culture. The nearby West Kennet long barrow with all its Earth Mother symbolism was closed ritually and reverentially during the period of Silbury's construction. Perhaps that is evidence of a fond farewell to the old Goddess icons and to a social structure that must have engendered a spirit of co-operation and mutual understanding. If that had not been the case, the Stonehenge bluestones could not have been safely transported all the way from Pembrokeshire, and people would not have brought livestock from as far as Orkney for the winter celebrations at Durrington Walls and Stonehenge. There would be no Silbury Hill or Avebury henge. Such time-consuming projects could only have been undertaken with the support of communities from very wide areas, and would have been inconceivable if there had been any threat of hostility. It may not have been an era of the complete peace and harmony of a truly 'golden' age, but we have certainly not experienced anything like it since. Our Neolithic landscapes and monuments, especially the magnificent Silbury Hill, stand as testament that the Great Goddess was indeed the deity of the original British civilisation. For all those whom always believed so, I hope this book provides some measure of vindication.

Appendix

For the sun, there are sixteen salient alignments to consider. These are the rising and setting points for the Summer and Winter Solstices, the Spring and Autumn Equinoxes and the pagan festival days of Beltane, Lughnasa, Samain and Imbolc. The festivals are traditionally held on days considered to be the half-way point between a solstice and an equinox. Although a matter of some debate concerning the correct terminology, the festivals are referred to here as quarter days.

In 2500 BC, the rising Summer Solstice sun's upper limb (the tip) was at a declination of 24.25°. At Silbury's latitude of 51.41° north, the sun's azimuth or angle on the horizon was 48.8° from true north when calculated on a flat horizon with 0° elevation. When corrected for the actual elevation of the horizon and for atmospheric refraction, the first flash of the sun seen from Silbury Hill occurred at 49.2°. That is on the near horizon formed by the Ridgeway, but not at a point of the skyline that forms a noticeable notch or pinnacle, and not above any monument or marker. Neither is there anything notable about the sun's setting azimuth of 312.4°.

As there are 365.25 days in a year, and counting the number of days from Summer Solstice, the May quarter day Beltane is a mean number of 319.59 days from Solstice, and the August quarter day Lughnasa is 45.66 days. Of course there can never be a fraction of a sunrise, so the sunrises that most accurately indicate the festivals are 320 days (usually May 7th) and 46 days (August 6th). The corrected azimuth for the May quarter day is 62.5°, which aligns with the Ridgeway approximately 1.5 kms NNE of the former Sanctuary stone circle. Again there is nothing of note in that part of the skyline. The setting azimuth of 298.8° is very close to a tumulus slightly to the north of Knoll Down, but in an area so rich in tumuli of various ages that is hardly surprising. The August quarter day sunrise was at 61.5°, only 1° away from the May alignment on the Ridgeway, and the sunset was at 299.8°, again just 1° from May's apparently insignificant sector of the skyline.

Most of the formulae used in these calculations are taken from Professor Clive Ruggles' *Astronomy in Prehistoric Britain and*

Ireland (Yale University Press 1999), in which he wrote that for various reasons the equinoxes would not have been easily recognisable or of any great interest to the Neolithic population. Nevertheless, for the record, the mean number of days from Summer Solstice for the Spring Equinox is 273.94 days, so day 274 is closest. The Autumn Equinox is at 91.31 days, so day 91 has been chosen. The corrected sunrise azimuth for day 274 is 88.39°, which is the very long alignment with Forest Hill's skyline slightly beyond Marlborough, but it does not mark the point where Silbury's eastern sightlines break from the very close horizon of the Ridgeway. It is around 2° south of the horizon break, which would represent a misalignment of up to four days; too great an error for people who could easily have counted the days from Summer Solstice. The sunset was at 270.4° on Cherhill Down's eastern spur, and once again in an unremarkable location. As less than 0.2° separates the Autumn Equinox alignments from Spring's, both are in practically identical positions.

The solar clock comes around to the next special sunrises of Samain and Imbolc. Theoretically, the November quarter day Samain is 136.96 days from Summer Solstice, and February's Imbolc is 228.28 days. 137 days is usually November 5th, and 228 days is February 4th. On day 137 the corrected sunrise occurred at 117.7°, which is above West Woods and nowhere near any monuments, horizon breaks, notches or pinnacles. The sunset was at 242.3° on a very close and insignificant horizon near Beckhampton Penning. The corrected sunrise azimuth for day 228 was 116.4° in West Woods, and the sunset was at 243.6° on Bishop's Canning Down, which once again does not appear significant.

Winter Solstice completes the set of special solar days. An observer on Silbury Hill would have seen it rise at 130.4° above Huish Hill, high on the southern escarpment. However, that is not the highest point of the escarpment, and the skyline contains nothing of interest. The sunset was at 230.2°, which is exactly on a break in the horizon between the near Beckhampton Penning and the distant Horton Down. There are many horizon breaks in that sector, none of which appear remarkable in any way.

There still remains the question of possible lunar alignments with the full moon's Major and Minor extremes. The Northern Major moon would have been seen to rise at 40.8°. That is close to the highest visible point of the Ridgeway, although not close enough to have been the intention. The setting point was at 321.1°, which could be close to the northernmost visible sector of the Cotswold Hills. I calculate that point to have been at approximately 319°, but it would require a survey far beyond my technical abilities to be sure. The Northern Minor moon rose at 59.9° above the non-descript horizon of the Ridgeway, and set at 301.4°. That is far from the Cotswold Hill's southernmost visible sector, which I calculate to have been at 307.7°.

The Southern Minor moon rose at 122° above the distant eastern slope of Martinsell Hill, and very close to the Iron Age hillfort. Martinsell Hill forms a prominent pinnacle on the horizon, and as the moon continued to rise, its full disc would then have appeared at 123.3°, exactly above the highest point of the hill and in the centre of the fort. Some hillforts were built on earlier Neolithic sites, and that could have been interesting if there had been any other alignments on a similar theme, but there simply are not. The setting point was at 238.2° on Bishop's Canning Down. The Southern Major moon rose at 143.3° above Golden Ball Hill, setting at 216.5° above the southern escarpment, and none of those alignments appear to have any significance whatsoever.

With only one possible 'hit' from a potential twenty-four, I think it is safe to say that Silbury Hill was not designed as an astronomical observatory.

Bibliography

Ashe, G. *King Arthur's Avalon.* Collins. 1957.

Atkins, W. S. (Consultants.) *Kennet and Coln river levels study. Final report, volume one – River Kennet.* For the National Rivers Authority. 1992.

Atkinson, R.J.C. in Ruggles, C. L. N., Whittle, J.W.R. (eds) *Astronomy and Society in Britain during the period 4000-1500 BC.* British Archaeological Reports. Vol 88. 1981.

Barker, C.T. *The Long Mounds of the Avebury Region.* Wiltshire Archaeological and Natural History Magazine. Vol 79. 1985 pp. 7-38.

Brown, G., Field, D., McOmish, D. (eds.) *The Avebury Landscape.* Oxbow. 2005.

Burl, A. *The Stone circles of Britain, Ireland and Brittany.* Yale University Press. 2000.

Burl, A. *Prehistoric Avebury.* Yale University Press. 2002.

Burl, A. *A Guide To the Stone Circles of Britain, Ireland and Brittany.* Yale University Press. 1995.

Chippendale, C. *Stonehenge Complete (new and expanded edition.)* Thames and Hudson. 2004.

Cleal, R., Walker, K., Montague, R. *Stonehenge in its Landscape: Twentieth Century Excavations.* English Heritage Archaeological Report 10. 1995.

Cope, J. *The Modern Antiquarian.* Thorsons. 1998.

Cope, J. *The Megalithic European.* Element. 2004.

Cunliffe, B., Renfrew, C. (eds) *Science and Stonehenge.* Oxford University Press. 1997.

Curtis, M.R., and G.R. *Callanish. Stones, Moon and Sacred Landscape.* Self published. 1994.

Dames, M. *The Silbury Treasure.* Thames and Hudson. 1976.

Dames, M. *Silbury. Resolving the Enigma.* The History Press. 2010.

Devereux, P. (in) Antiquity 65. 1991 pp. 894-8.

Darvill, T.C. *Stonehenge, the biography of a landscape.* Tempus. 2006.

Evans, J.G., Whittle, A.R.W., Gardiner, J. *An environmental History of the Upper Kennet Valley, Wiltshire for the last 10,000 years.* Proceedings of the Prehistoric Society 59. 1993 pp. 139-195.

Field, D. *Great Sites. Silbury Hill.* British Archaeology. May 2003.

Field, D., Brown, G., Crockett, A. *The Marlborough Mount Revisited.* Wiltshire Archaeological & Natural History Magazine, vol 94. 2001. pp. 195-204.

Gillings, M., Pollard, J. *Avebury.* Duckworth. 2004.

Gimbutas, M. *The Language of the Goddess.* Thames and Hudson. 1989.

Goodison, L., Morris, C. (eds.) *Ancient Goddesses.* British Museum Press. 1998.

Harding, J. *Henge Monuments of the British Isles.* Tempus. 2003.

Hawkes, J. *God in the machine.* Antiquity 41. 1967.

Hawkins, G., White, J. *Stonehenge Decoded.* Souvenir Press. 1966.

Leary, J., Field, D. *The Story of Silbury Hill.* English Heritage. 2010.

Leary, J., Field, D., Campbell, G. (eds.) *Silbury Hill. The largest prehistoric mound in Europe.* English Heritage. 2013.

Lockyer, N. *Stonehenge and other British Monuments Astronomically considered.* Macmillan. 1909.

Marshall, P. *Europe's Lost Civilisation.* Headline. 2004.

Marshall, S. *Silbury. Spring.* British Archaeology Issue 131. (July/August) 2013.

Meaden, T. *The Secrets of the Avebury Stones.* Souvenir Press. 1999.

Miller, H., Broadhurst, P. *The Sun and The Serpent.* Pendragon Press. 1989.

Moffat, A. *Before Scotland.* Thames and Hudson. 2005.

Mortimer, N. *Stukeley Illustrated.* Green Magic. 2003.

Newham, C.A. *The Astronomical significance of Stonehenge.* Coates and Parker. 2000.

North, J. *Stonehenge. Neolithic Man and the Cosmos.* Harper Collins. 1996.

Parker Pearson, M. *Stonehenge.* Simon and Schuster. 2012
.
Parker Pearson, M., Ramilisonina. *Stonehenge for the ancestors: the stones pass on the message.* Antiquity 72. 1998.

Pitts, M. *Hengeworld.* Century. 2000.

Pollard, J., Ruggles, C. L. N. *Shifting Perceptions.* Cambridge Archaeological Journal 11:1. 2001. pp. 69-90.

Pryor, F. *Britain BC.* Harper Collins. 2003.

Rahtz, P., Watts, L. *Glastonbury Myth & Archaeology.* Tempus. 2003.

Respondek, L. *The Mystery of Silbury Hill.* Elar. 2005.

Ruggles, C. L. N. *Astronomy in Prehistoric Britain and Ireland.* Yale University Press. 1999.

Russell, M. *Monuments of the British Neolithic.* Tempus. 2002.

Smith, I. *Windmill Hill and Avebury: Excavations by A. Keiller 1925-29.* Oxford Clarendon Press. 1965.

Ucko, P. J., Hunter, M., Clark, A. J., David, A. *Avebury Reconsidered.* London. 1991.

Whittle, A. *Sacred Mound, Holy Rings.* Oxbow. 1997.

Whittle, A., Pollard, J., Grigson, C. *The Harmony of Symbols.* Oxbow. 1999.

INDEX

Aberdeenshire   119, 121, 122
Adam (stone)   10, 42
Adam's Grave   38
Atkinson, Richard   14-17, 20, 21, 27, 30, 34, 40, 51, 52, 62, 64, 65, 67, 72, 124
Aubrey, John   8, 9
Avebury   4, 6-10, 13, 23, 25, 26, 28, 36, 38, 42, 69, 78, 82, 83, 87, 106, 127
Avebury henge   3, 4, 16, 25-27, 31, 33, 38, 43, 81, 82, 128
Balbirnie   117, 118
Balfarg   117, 118
Barton Down   57, 60
Bathurst Deane, John   13
BBC   15, 16, 21, 100
Beacon Hill   88, 89, 91, 92, 94
Beaker   104, 105
Beckhampton Avenue   10, 28, 42, 44, 45
Beckhampton long barrow   26
Beckhampton Penning   130
Beltane   27, 129
Best, Joanne   58, 59
Bishop's Canning Down   50, 130, 131
Black Combe   113
Blandford, Henry   12, 13
Bodmin Moor   108
Brentor   109, 110
Bridport   101, 103
Broadhurst, Paul   27, 28, 45
Burl, Aubrey   34, 58, 72, 75, 110, 115, 117, 119, 120
Callanish   32, 73-77, 113, 126
Camden, William   115
Carn Brae   105-107
Castle Hill   100
Castlerigg   112
Chadburn, Amanda   40, 80

Cheesewring   108, 109
Cherhill Down   60, 130
Clay Mound   88, 89, 92, 94
Cleal, Rosemund   26, 36
Cley Hill   104
Cnoc an Tursa   75-77
Colmer's Hill   101, 103
Colt Hoare, Sir Richard   38
Coneybury Hill   95, 96
Cope, Julian   6, 7, 32, 33, 37, 55, 58, 69, 75, 77, 101, 104, 113,
1119, 121, 127
Corfe Castle   81
Cornwall   28, 100, 105
Cotswolds   50, 69
Cotsworth, Moses   33, 34
Cowie, John   34
Crickley Hill   105
Cumbria   6, 71, 112, 115
Curtis, Bill   16
Curtis, Margaret   75-77
Dames, Michael   6, 7, 28-31, 55, 107, 125
Dartmoor   110, 122
Devereux, Paul   25-27, 41
Devil's Den   2, 39
Doghouse Hill   102
Dorset   10, 101, 102, 105
Down Tor   111, 112
Drax, Edward   10-12
Duggleby Howe   34
Dunnideer Hill   119, 121
Durrington Walls   54, 71, 82, 83, 88, 90, 96, 128
Easter Aquhorthies   119, 120
Edmunds, Mike   55
Equinox   129, 130
Evans et al   41, 51-53
Eve (stone)   10, 42
Falkner, Richard   12, 13

Falkner's Circle   42, 44
Fergusson, James   13
Field, David   50, 54, 58, 63-65, 67, 68, 72, 106, 124
Folly Hill   32
Forest Hill   130
Fox Covert   28
Giant's Grave   113
Gimbutas, Marija   6, 107
Glastonbury Tor   85-87
Goggleby Stone   115, 116
Golden Ball Hill   131
Golden Cap   101-103
Granham Hill   82
Greater Cursus   94
Great Trilithon   96, 97
Grooved Ware   97
Hambledon Hill   101, 102, 105
Harestone Down   42, 44, 72, 78, 79
Harris   74, 126
Hart-Jones, Barbara   21
Hecatus of Abdera   74
Heelstone   3, 95
Hill of Christ's Kirk   119
Hill of Flinder   119
Hill of Skulls   115, 117
Horton Down   130
Hoy   97, 98, 100
Huish Hill   130
Hurlers   108, 109
Imbolc   129, 130
Janssen, Bert   22
Jones, Arthur   11
Joseph, Chris   53
Kemp Howe   115, 116,
Kidsty Pike   116
Kilmartin   122
King Barrow Ridge   88, 89, 92, 95

King Sil   5, 8, 9
King's Play Hill   50
King's Play long barrow   39
Knap Hill   69, 70, 72
Knoll Down   27, 28, 45, 129
Leary, Jim   63-65, 67, 72, 106, 124
Lewis   74, 75, 77
Leyland   50
Littlebredy   101
Loanhead of Daviot   120, 121
Long Bredy   101
Long Hill   100, 101
Long Meg   112
Longstones   42, 44
Lubbock, John   15
Lughnasa   27, 129
Maes Howe   35, 97-99
Manton Down   57, 60
Marlborough   46, 48, 49, 53, 57-59, 69, 81, 130
Marlborough Mount   57-60, 68, 81-83, 124, 125
Marshall, Steve   50, 55, 125
Martinsell Hill   131
Matheson, Sir James   74
McKim, F.R.   15
Meaden, Terence   78
Mere   100
Merewether, John   12, 13, 17
Milk Hill   69, 71, 78
Miller, Hamish   27, 28, 45
Mither Tap   119-122
Moffat, Alistair   2, 86, 119
Morgan's Hill   50, 60
Ness of Brodgar   97, 98, 100
Neumann, Erich   107
Northern Major   32, 95, 131
Northern Minor   131
Obelisk   43, 44

Old Bath Road   45
Oliver, Neil   100
Orkney   35, 54, 71, 97, 98, 100, 128
Ossebard, Janet   22
Parker Pearson, Mike   88, 90, 91, 98, 100, 127
Pass, Alfred   11, 14, 51
Pecked Hill   69, 70, 72, 73, 78, 85, 124
Petrie, Flinders   15, 65
Pitts, Mike   23, 106
Pollard, Joshua   32, 96
Primary mound   25, 30, 51, 63-65, 68
Pryor, Francis   105
Pytheas   74, 77
Respondek, Lothar   34
Ridgeway   38, 45, 46, 49, 57, 61, 69, 82, 129-131
Ring of Brodgar   97, 100
River Avon   82, 89
River Bride   101
River Brit   101
River Kennet   4, 9, 48-50, 55-57, 59, 82, 83
River Og   48, 82
Robin Hood's Ball   87, 88
Rockley Down   38
Rogers, Dr   59
Roughridge Hill long barrow   38
Roundway Hill   46, 48, 49, 50
Ruggles, Clive   96, 129
Russel, Miles   37-39
Samain   129, 130
Sanctuary   10, 26, 28, 42, 44, 45, 72, 78, 79, 82, 106, 129
Siculus, Diodurus   74
Shap   115
Skellow Hill   115
Skye   74
Sleeping Beauty   75, 76, 78, 113, 126
Smith, Isobel   72
Southern Major   32, 73, 75, 95, 131

Southern Minor   95, 131
Stonehenge   3, 4, 6-8, 15, 21, 26, 42, 54, 71, 82, 83, **87-90**, 92, 94-97, 100, 128
Stones of Stennes   97
Stukeley, William   **8-10**, 13, 28, 42, 43, 78, 79
Summer Solstice   3, 32, 89, 91, 94, 95, 129, 130
Swallowhead Springs   9, 50-52
Swinside   113, 114
Tan Hill   69
Tap O'Noth   119, 121, 122
Taylor, John   16
Thunder Stone   115, 116
Toland, John   74
Totterdown   49, 60
Two Waters   126
Vale of Pewsey   69, 73, 80
Waden Hill   23, 26, 27, 38, 43-45, 56, 69-73, 78-82, 124, 125
Wansdyke   69
West Kennet Avenue   28, 42, 44, 45, 82
West Kennet long barrow   36, 37, 127
West Overton formation   51, 53
West Woods   130
Wheatley, Maria   28
Whitehead, Paul   55
Whitesheet Hill   100, 101
Whittle, Alasdair   18, 19, 21, 25, 29, 34, 42, 52, 72
Willy Howe   34
Windmill Hill   4, 32, 41, 43, 45, 72, 73, 80, 106
Winterbourne   4, 46, 51, 53, 81
Winterbourne Basset circle   42, 44, 78
Winter Solstice   3, 23, 32, 54, 89, 91, 94, 96-98, 129, 130
Wold Newton   34
Woodborough Hill   69-73, 78, 124
Woodhenge   88, 95, 96
Z-feature   26